PADMAVAT

AN EPIC LOVE STORY

Praise for Padamavat: An Epic Love Story

"Purushottam Agrawal is a new age master of medieval Hindi literature.... Agrawal lays out [his central theme] with great élan and very wide-ranging scholarship. [His] Padmavat stands out as a profound challenge to much received wisdom.'

—Harbans Mukhia in *The Wire*

'Few literary scholars understand history, and even fewer historians have an appreciation of literature. In this superb study of a great, if somewhat neglected, epic, Professor Purushottam Agrawal seamlessly bridges literature and history, past and present, politics and emotions. I read the book at one stretch, enthralled and absorbed, learning many small things and one large lesson; that early modern poetry is vastly superior to postmodern cinema, both in terms of aesthetic beauty as well as historical truth.'

—Ramachandra Guha

'An "in-depth analysis" and what is called "an easy read" are generally seen as incompatible. It is a rare combination. However, Purushottam Agrawal has achieved this deftly in his deeply insightful commentary on *Padmavat*. In transparent language he captures and analyses the mileu of Malik Muhammad Jayasi's epic poem, *Padmavat*. He tells us how "masnavi", a classical genre of Persian poetry, the doha (couplet), chaupaii (quartet) of Awadhi, the praise of Allah and his Prophet and the miracles of Lord Shiva and Parvati are an intrinsic part of the same narrative. He shows us how history, mythology, imagination and fantasy merge together to form a seamless epic. Purushottam Agrawal embraces tradition and modernity with equal felicity. He has the heart of a lover and the mind of a scholar. Again, a rare combination.'

—Javed Akhtar

'Padmavat, a great epic of Jayasi, has been critically presented by Purushottam Agrawal in a manner in which robust scholarship, contextual analysis and the epical dimensions are imaginatively fused to create a lucid and readable text. All epics universally combine history, racial memory, popular legends and fantasy: Padmavat does this in no small measure. In the current popular readings and interpretations it is important to assert and emphasize that Padmavat is a brilliant and classical act of imagination and not a historical chronicle and must be read and appreciated as a creative text—a monument of poetic magnificence.

It celebrates memorably love and beauty making them inevitable dimensions of truth more enduring than so-called historical truth. Purushottam Agrawal has done service to a great poet, his times and his creative imagination by putting them all in proper and critical perspective.
It is important appreciate that *Padmavat* is neither "a bardic poem valorizing any of the conflicting parties". It is a tropic tale of love of epic proportions with immense "humanizing poignancy".'

—Ashok Vajpeyi

'A strangely gripping book. You feel you're part of an adventure, guided by an old, obscure poet. You're in search of meaning, and in constant dialogue with our times.'

—Krishna Kumar

'This book is a guided tour through Jayasi's poem, lucid, easy to read, informative without being pedantic, matter of fact rather than declamatory; his observations always to the point, while his regular quotations from the work, with accompanying translation, open a window to what must be a marvellous text, still awaiting readers.'

—Vijay Tankha in *The Tribune*

Purushottam Agrawal delves into this little known poem and provides a commentary for the interested. He sets Jayasi's work in its context.

—Anjana Basu in *The Statesman*

PADMAVAT

AN EPIC LOVE STORY

PURUSHOTTAM AGRAWAL

Introduced & Illustrated by

DEVDUTT PATTANAIK

RUPA

Published by
Rupa Publications India Pvt. Ltd 2018
7/16, Ansari Road, Daryaganj
New Delhi 110002

Sales centres:

Allahabad Bengaluru Chennai
Hyderabad Jaipur Kathmandu
Kolkata Mumbai

ISBN: 978-93-5304-023-9

Second impression 2018

10 9 8 7 6 5 4 3 2

Design and typeset in Garamond by Special Effects Graphics Design Co, Mumbai

Printed by Parksons Graphics Pvt. Ltd., Mumbai

For Ritambhara and Ritwik,
and their generation

Contents

Love and Beauty for the Lazy Mind

Devdutt Pattanaik

Is Rani Padmini of Chittor fact or fiction? The answer depends on who is asked.

Padmini is definitely fact for a Rajput, especially one for whom identity matters in a social context. She is most likely fiction for a historian who has no skin in the game. This makes the tale a myth: true for the insider, false for the outsider, very much like the idea of God—true for the believer, false for the non-believer. If fact is everybody's truth and fiction is nobody's truth, then myth is somebody's truth, a subjective truth of a people, inherited over generations, shaped by stories, symbols and rituals venerated by clan, caste, class and community. Subjective truths serve as a glue to bind people together. Questioning their validity threatens the collective.

The story of Padmini is a special kind of myth. It is legend, firmly anchored in history and geography, in fourteenth-century Chittor, very different from pure myths such as the story of the God of Abraham whose Eden cannot be located in time and space (though attempts have been made). Insiders, or believers, will always find evidence to establish their claims. Outsiders—the non-believers, the sceptics—will always point out that these 'facts' demand a leap of faith. This angers the faithful, as it rattles the keystones of their identity. If there is no God, what happens to claims of being a Chosen People and claims over a Promised Land? Likewise, if there is no Padmini, what happens to tales of Rajput valour and pride? Are they all fantasy, propaganda? The anger is understandable.

Politicians exploit this anger in order to harvest a vote bank, which is the currency of survival in a democracy. It explains the rise of right-wing groups in recent times across the world. People want an identity; they refuse to be reduced to mere humans, which is the logical extension of humanist philosophies that shape modern societies. They want to be British, and American, and Indian, and Rajput, and Brahmin, and not be made ashamed of their identity.

Yet mocking identity is exactly what the Left does, with its doctrine of equality and social justice: continuously providing evidence that transforms glorious peoples into a collective of privileged 'oppressors'. Truths such as these have all the appearances of being objective, but they are part of a political agenda to strip clans and communities of the special status they grant themselves in the effort to spark an Armageddon-like revolution that will create an imagined utopia. So while left-leaning politicians harness votes from the 'oppressed', right-leaning politicians harness votes from the 'oppressor'. Each one insists they speak the truth. Each one insists they are objective and accuses the other of fake news. Battle lines are thus drawn.

The battle over Padmini, or God, is a battle of identity, of culture, of a way of being, and not a battle over facts. It is a battle of whose subjectivity matters. Is the truth the narrative of the insider, who the outsider identifies as 'oppressor' or the narrative of the outsider, who self-identifies himself or herself with the 'oppressed' and as a 'truth-seeker'? It is a battle of lazy minds who refuse to see the role of imagination in human life.

Lazy minds are minds that find comfort in binaries. They hate the idea of myth that shape-shifts as fact or fiction depending on the observer. They prefer the fixed to the fluid, the material to the psychological, and the literal to the metaphorical. They prefer argument or vi-vaad to discussion or sam-vaad, as they are more interested in being right than in expanding their perspective of things. They view subjectivity as a contamination. In seeking to establish the primacy of a single truth, which is often confused with objectivity, lazy minds reject the simultaneous existence of multiple narratives, each one catering to a different audience, each one satisfying a different agenda.

India, and the world, has ended up nurturing too many lazy minds in the quest for a scientific temper. We have, without realizing it, given primacy to objectivity over subjectivity, to critical thinking over critical empathy, to engineering and mathematics over literature and arts. This puritanical approach has resulted in the humanities being taught as social 'science', mimicking the study of material science. So art appreciation simply ends up becoming an exercise in uncovering 'facts' of underlying political and economic motives, with scant attention paid to the insecurities and inspirations that inspired the 'myth' in the first place and made it popular. This over-reliance on the scientific temper is why only the historian's truth takes centre stage, and there is scant regard for the truth of philosophers and poets.

Bards, poets and film-makers have long known that to be successful one's work has to acknowledge the subjective truth of one's patron, or one's audience. So when we study a work of art, we can get a peep into the mind of the people who produced the art, who consumed the art, and who made it a success. The success of a Bollywood magnum opus on Padmini, for example, reveals neither a record of events that took place in the fourteenth century, nor a faithful recreation of the sixteenth-century literary classic, but a reflection of twenty-first-century thirst to demonize Muslims and glamourize a beautiful woman who burns herself for her honour and the honour of her husband and his clan. Had the film been rejected by the masses, it would have told us something else. Does the film's reception reveal a reaction of contemporary Indian audiences to the intellectual fetishization of Islam, the rising trend of man-hating and tradition-bashing used to justify gender equality? These are discomforting but important questions the film provokes and we need to ponder on. The lazy mind, however, will ignore these questions and insist on seeing films either as propaganda, or the truth.

Popular oral history, like any successful Bollywood film, gives a glimpse into the minds of the people who kept demanding an encore. Eight hundred years ago, it was important for Rajput bards to celebrate Rajput valour by singing of warriors and their brides, who chose death by steel, or fire, to dishonour. For it was clear, they were no match for the rising tide of new invaders from the north-west, identified then as Turks, identified now as Muslims. In battle after battle, the Rajputs were losing. How does one prop up the self-worth of a people facing defeat? Surely not by describing the battles objectively, or by castigating the losers. Rather by demonizing the enemy, making them sneaky rather than brave, while simultaneously establishing heroes and, moreover, heroes who choose death over surrender and captivity.

Similar tales were told before, even before the foreign invaders appeared on the scene, when the villain was a neighbouring king, often a rival clan member. But over time, narratives of war with outsiders overshadowed narratives of war with insiders, resonating the Indian preference for the epic Ramayana where the hero fights the rakshasas, to the Mahabharata where the heroes fight their own cousins. Bards realized that their audience valued Rajputs, who chose death, to those who established peace through marriage and service with Mughal royalty, which explains why there are more stories in Rajput lore of women burning themselves than of women being turned into peace offerings.

In oral history, as in Bollywood extravaganzas, the battle is rarely political or economic; it is always moral. The villains are jealous, or lustful, or greedy, or intolerant of other faiths. Many modern historians have earned the ire of Hindus for dismissing oral history as fantasy and for favouring the argument that the Islamic invasion of India had nothing to do with Islamic morality, but everything to do with the quest of Central Asian Turks for wealth and power. The destruction of Hindu temples, an integral part of Hindu lore, is reduced to exaggerated propaganda, and battles long considered religious wars, a violent organized rejection of Hindu image worship, are being categorized, even justified, as secular plunder. This becomes, for many, yet another case of fetishization of Islam, an affliction of modern academia that seems to be increasingly leaning towards the Left. It provided rich fodder to the Right.

For centuries, the most famous literary epic poem on Padmini was Malik Muhammad Jayasi's *Padmavat*, composed in the sixteenth century. What did its success in its time reveal about the mind of the audience? To find out, we have to be thankful to Prof. Purushottam Agrawal for writing this brilliant and highly accessible commentary. Reading this book helped me appreciate an India that existed 500 years ago, an India that was not medieval, but modern.

The adjective 'modern' means the desire to engage with, and mix with, different ideas, rather than violently rejecting them for fear of contamination. Sixteenth-century India was willing to engage with foreign ideas which is why Jayasi's work written in the Gangetic plains in Awadhi, a dialect of Hindi, retells a story of Rajasthani bards, using idioms and metaphors both from the world of Islam, and from the world of Hindu Puranas. This is quite a contrast from sixteenth-century Europe where Anti-Semitism and Islamophobia was widespread, Catholic Christians were at war with Protestant Christians, and the Church was coming down heavily on 'witches' and scientists. Indeed contemporary

India, where religious, secular or nationalistic outrage lurks like a rabid dog in every corner, seems more akin to medieval Europe than Jayasi's early modern India.

Prof. Agrawal demonstrates how this poem has nothing to do with history, religion, or God, or hatred, or invasions, or honour. We find no trace of the right-wing's 'thousand years of slavery' discourse or the left-wing's 'Brahmanical hegemony' discourse. It is simply an incredible ode to love, where characters happen to be Rajput, Brahmin and Muslim. Their nobility or cupidity is a function of their personality, not their identity.

More importantly, Prof. Agrawal helps us appreciate how Jayasi's work celebrates womanhood and makes a virtue of eroticism (shringara rasa). We realize how the poet was challenging the male-centric monastic view of the time, where giving up women is valorized and appreciating women is equated with weakness and moral decay. Indeed those who insist on seeing Jayasi's work as a mystical Sufi allegory, come across as puritans, who are discomforted by beauty and embarrassed by desire.

Prof. Agrawal traces the themes in the epic poem to Jayasi's physical 'ugliness' and the resultant sense of rejection and low-esteem. The imagination of Padmini's perfect beauty helps Jayasi rise above bitterness and misery. He yearns to be Ratansen, who pines for her, and is willing to die for her, not Devpal or Khilji who seek to possess her by force, with no regard for her wishes. This regard for consent reaffirms the modernity of Jayasi just as the projection of her death as martyrdom in the face of invading contamination reveals the medieval mindset of contemporary times.

Devdutt Pattanaik

Today, as technology is being used to amplify ugliness we need to relook at Jayasi's poem, which elevates us towards love and beauty. Love and beauty are not the concern of 'realists' who are obsessed with wealth and power. Jayasi's poem is for those whose mind is not too lazy to enquire deeper into the human condition, empathize with the fear and hunger that propels it, and love and beauty that nourishes it.

I am grateful to Prof. Agrawal for enabling me to immerse myself in Jayasi's *Padmavat*. It inspired me to embellish his text with my illustrations. May it expand your mind too. And as you peep into the world of your ancestors, try not to fall into the trap of fact and fiction by constantly reminding yourself:

Within infinite myths lies an eternal truth
Who sees it all?
Varuna has but a thousand eyes
Indra, a hundred
You and I only two.

Author's Note

Padmavat, contrary to popular perception, is not a Sufi allegory. It is *not* aimed at luring the reader in the name of a love story and then giving her a tutorial in Sufism. The stanza that supposedly provides the 'key' to understanding the Sufi allegory nature of *Padmavat* was inserted into it centuries after its composition. This fact has been known for decades; no serious scholar takes *Padmavat* as an allegory any more.

It is also not a call to arms in the name of community honour. Love is primary in Malik Muhammad Jayasi's *Padmavat*—battle only secondary. Unlike his 'modern readers', the poet is not obsessed with the conflict between his hero and the Sultan of

Delhi. More than two-thirds of his epic is about that epitome of beauty—Padmavati, and Ratansen's sadhana for her. Jayasi does not even let his hero die in the battle with Alauddin.

Jayasi was not the kind of poet who would reduce human beings into lifeless symbols and the story to a dry religious discourse; or a call to arms. He was, of course a revered Sufi, but his *Padmavat* is not Sufi propaganda tract. In this poignant epic, far from suffering a dose of dry discourses, you come across people trying to come to terms with the vagaries of love and life in general.

Jayasi's sympathies are clearly with Ratansen, not because he is a Hindu warrior, but because is a love-yogi. Jayasi's Alauddin is cunning and unfair to Padmavati and Ratansen, yet he is not a monster. Jayasi's characters are not just good guys or bad guys. His *Padmavat* is first-rate poetry, not an opulent, regressive Bollywood extravaganza.

Jayasi never meant to write history. His poem is a work of creative, imaginative literature woven around an episode in history. He transforms that episode and its legend into a rich, intricate tapestry of love, desire, struggle and sacrifice. He places a local episode into a much wider cultural perspective and makes it the basis of a classic through his vast knowledge of mythology and folklore. He constantly alludes to Hindu and Islamic mythology and legends, in particular to Hindu ones. His knowledge of Hindu mythology in its various tellings is so deep and rich, and his deployment of the same so appropriate that you cannot but feel awe for the unique combination of poetic and scholarly excellence in his epic.

Jayasi had, like many of his contemporaries, a clear geographical sense of India. On many occasions he uses the phrase हेम सेत, गौर गजना—from Himalayas to the Ocean; from Bengal to

Ghazni (present-day Afghanistan). He was a devout Muslim and a proud Indian.

The essence of his own life experiences speaks silently between the lines in his celebration of the pleasure and pain of erotic love and its potential of turning human into divine.

And he is neither the first nor the last to celebrate love and erotic desire in this way. He is unique, but not alone. Indian tradition has been mature enough not to be prudish about erotic desire; it has celebrated and explored it instead. Jayasi is situated in this tradition. He wrote in Awadhi, spoken in eastern Uttar Pradesh; and is placed amongst the foremost writers in the history of Hindi literature. Not just the speakers of Hindi, but every Indian can be, rather ought to be, proud of Malik Muhammad Jayasi—the poet of *Padmavat.*

He belonged to his times. Like all of us do. But unlike most of us, he transcended his times by perceiving his surroundings in a refreshingly different way; by taking the leaps of creative imagination.

During the controversy around the film *Padmaavat*, Rajesh Jha of *India Today* asked me to write an essay. This essay, 'Theatre of Absurdity' (*India Today*, 4 Dec 2017), was well-received. Immediately after its publication, I received a message from my dear friend Devdutt Pattanaik, renowned for his innovative interpretations of mythology, asking me 'to write a little book about the real *Padmavat*'.

We had first met at the Jaipur Literature Festival, 2013. Devdutt heard me speak on a panel about the Kumbh Mela, and immediately sought me after the session. We met and instantly formed a mutual admiration society. Since then, Devdutt has asked me to write about many things and has suggested some very interesting themes as well.

But, this time, it was not a suggestion, but insistence—'People must know the real *Padmavat*,' Devdutt said.

He is right. Considering the nature and 'level' of most of the 'debates' around *Padmavat* these days, it is really important to know something about the real *Padmavat*, Jayasi's *Padmavat*.

I have been researching on the early modernity of India—which manifests itself in so-called vernacular languages—for some decades. Kabir has been at the centre of my explorations and reflections, but, Jayasi and others have also been part and parcel of my research.

I taught Jayasi's *Padmavat* to postgraduate students of Hindi literature at the Jawaharlal Nehru University in New Delhi. That was more than twenty years ago. I recall with nostalgia the impact of my lectures on the students and remember those young women and men fondly. As a matter of fact, since my own postgraduate student days, I have been in love with *Padmavat,* composed by a poetic genius who had no sight in one eye and was hard of hearing in one ear; who was acutely conscious of his 'ugly' appearance and justly confident of his poetic talent.

If you can read Awadhi and consider poetry as something more than a mere pastime, have some existential concerns and value love in your life; you are bound to be as enamoured of *Padmavat* as I am. I feel happy and deeply satisfied for having been able to reflect in a structured way on a poet, to whom I am deeply grateful. In fact, all of us ought to be. I feel very strongly that it would greatly help to build a saner society if we listened more attentively to poets like Jayasi, and I sincerely hope that after reading this book, you will not find this statement hyperbolic.

I also hope these reflections on *Padmavat*—a love story par excellence—will help the reader gain a better sense of the claims and conflicts of love in general as well as the one in her or his life.

The numbering of stanzas quoted in this book refers to Vasudev Sharan Agrawal's edition of *Padmavat* (1980, Jhansi).

Historical or not, Jayasi's Padmavati has become 'more than real'. I too am more than grateful to Devdutt Pattanaik for 'forcing' me back to Jayasi, and also for agreeing to illustrate this book.

I have also briefly reflected here on a very important poetic work, *Chhitai Charit*, which contains the only pre-Jayasi literary reference to 'Padmini of Chittor'. This rare work, unfortunately, has not received the attention it deserves. Pt. Harihar Niwas Dwivedi in collaboration with Sh. Agar Chand Nahta published a good edition of this important text in 1960. I am working on it, and hope to publish a translation with a critical introduction soon. I am grateful to my friends Rituraj Dwivedi and Jayant Tomar for making it available to me. Dr. Mata Prasad Gupta had also published an edition of this work.

My thanks are due to Mita Kapur of Siyahi.

I am grateful to Simar Puneet for her editorial suggestions.

I am grateful to my student Kundan Yadav, an officer of Indian Revenue Service, for his continuous support and witty, poignant reflections on the realities of life.

My gratitude to my wife—Suman Keshari, a brilliant poet—is not confined to help provided for this book and certainly cannot be expressed by words alone.

Ritambhara, a budding writer, photographer and aspiring film-maker, my daughter; and her elder brother Ritwik, a true scholar, intellectual and philosopher; and Neelakshi, a young, enthusiastic scholar; have always been providers of great inspiration.

And, of course, our kittens—Badka (sadly no more), Brownie,

Sotli and Chhutku—have provided me great opportunity to appreciate another idiom of love.

Purushottam Agrawal
New Delhi
February 2018

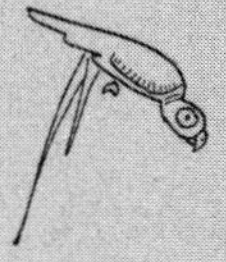

Introduction

Padmavat: An early modern epic

Padmavat is an epic about a woman. It is named after Padmavati, princess of Simhal, and not after her lover and husband, Ratansen—king of Chittor. Padmavati's friend, philosopher and guide is Hiraman—a parrot. Besides Padmavati there is also Nagmati—Ratansen's first wife. This tale of two women and their husband who are tormented by Alauddin Khalji is told by a man. Who was this man?

Malik Muhammad Jayasi (circa late-fifteenth–mid-sixteenth century CE) was one of the foremost poets of early modern vernacular literature in north India. Many people still insist on describing this period as 'medieval' as 'modernity' is supposed to have emerged in Indian history only as a result of colonial rule. But this view has been challenged over some decades by many historians, and now a large number of scholars prefer to describe the period from the fifteenth to the eighteenth century as 'early modern'.

To explain the point briefly—modernity is not merely about industrialization and fully evolved capitalism. As a matter of fact, the emergence of modern attitudes precedes industrialization and capitalism. Modernity is first reflected in the change of attitudes and the spread of commerce. Merchants and artisans look for avenues and openings in liberal outlooks. For instance, Dharamdas, one of the most important figures in the history of the Kabir Panth and the founder of one of its branches, was a merchant. Belief in rigid social hierarchies is challenged in favour of recognizing the inherent worth of every individual. The relationship of a human being not only with his/her immediate surrounding, but also with the universe and God is redefined. The spread of commerce leads to a weakening of exclusionist ideas of social behaviour. Attitudes towards tradition acquire a more reflective stance instead of a submissive one. The recognition of the worth of the individual, centrality of human principle and a re-evaluation of tradition—these are essential features of modernity. In the early modern era, even those who had a conservative attitude reworked traditional ideas. Tulsidas's idea of Ram Rajya is a case in point.

Modernity is not something which emerged only in Western Europe and was later exported to other parts of the world. In Europe, right at the beginning of the second millennium, the authority of the Roman Catholic Church was challenged by many 'millenarian' movements and uprisings. They were rooted in the Biblical forecasts of the return of Christ at the end of the millennium. These uprisings were brutally suppressed. But the Protestant movements led by Martin Luther and John Calvin in the sixteenth century proved too much for the Catholic Church to suppress. For literature and culture, the most important fallout of these movements was the rise of 'vernacular' languages as a medium of religious discourse. The Protestants translated the 'word of God' (the Bible) in people's languages, thus challenging the monopoly of the Latin-speaking elite over it. Simultaneously, there was a renaissance in the arts, reflecting and contributing to far-reaching changes in the social and cultural attitudes.

But, decreased influence of 'classical' and the rise of vernacular were not confined to Europe alone. 'Early modern' changes took place in other parts of the world almost simultaneously. China witnessed an unprecedented upsurge in vernacular creativity from the mid-fourteenth to mid-seventeenth centuries under the Ming dynasty. The intricate, classical poetic forms gave way to accessible and popular novels, short stories and travelogues. These works drew their themes not from royal lives but from the experiences of common people. There was more emphasis on psychological insights than on divine factors in descriptions of human emotions and situations. In Japan too, this period witnessed great innovations in art and literature. Haiku poetry, known worldwide today, developed during this period.

Keeping these changes in mind, the last millennium has been described as a 'Vernacular Millennium'. In India, traditional narratives reflecting cultural memories were reconstructed in vernacular languages. It is important to remember that *Ramcharitmanas* by Tulsidas, Adhyatama Ramayan (Malayalam) by Ezhuthachan or Mahabharata (Odia) by Sarala Das are not translations of Valmiki's Ramayana and Vyasa's Mahabharata. These, and other such works, are retellings of the age-old narratives in accordance with the temperament of the times. In their creative intent and thought-content, they are original works.

Unfortunately, we have internalized the colonial reconstruction of Indian history. As a result, we look at the second millennium as a period of intellectual stagnation or an 'age of commentaries', implying that hardly any new ideas of the individual, society, state and culture developed during this period. The fact of the matter is that a lot of new ideas grew and were circulated. To cite just one example, in this period, Krishna Deva Raya (1509–1530)—king of Vijyanagar—composed *Amuktamalyada* (in Telugu), containing reflections on the state and kingship.

'Vernacular Millennium' was a period of exciting intellectual and imaginative production in vernacular languages and in

Sanskrit and Persian. During this period, Indian commerce became so widespread that in the early eighteenth century, India had 22.6 per cent share of the global Gross Domestic Product; only China surpassed India in this respect. Such a strong and vibrant economy led to a major change in social attitudes; in other words, the emergence of early modernity. However, this early modernity could not grow much due to colonial intervention in Indian economy and society, which disrupted the indigenous potential of modernity and introduced the colonial version of European modernity instead.

Changes in attitude and world view are clearly perceptible in literary works, and records and documents of everyday practices in early modern India. The interrogation of caste prejudices (as in Kabir and Tukaram) or gender restrictions (as in Mira and Lal Ded) is reflective of an early modern attitude. More importantly, these voices were not lost in the wilderness; the contemporary society they evolved in provided them with a large number of eager listeners—even followers. Jayasi and other such poets also reflect the attitudes and concerns that were emerging in India's early modernity.

Ultimately, it is the individual's temperament and attitude that determines what kind of stance s/he will choose from the available ones. Even in our own times, not everyone shares an enthusiasm for 'modern' values like individual worth, openness of temperament, respect for 'difference', and so on. Similarly, the social context of early modern India does not in any way belittles the importance of the individual temperaments and choices of poets the likes of Kabir, Tulsi, Jayasi, Sur and Mira.

We will see as we explore Jayasi's Padmavat *more that his assessment of the characters depends on their individual acts and qualities, not on their religious backgrounds or ethnic identities. To him and to others like him, individuality was more important than the social, cultural and religious identity.*

Jayasi: The man and the poet

Jayasi's father was a mid-level village official, a 'malik' in the sultanate administration—hence the word *Malik* precedes the poet's given name. The word *Jayasi* in the name indicates that he belonged to Jayas town in the district of Amethi, Uttar Pradesh. Whether he was born there or migrated at a later point in his life has been a matter of debate amongst scholars. One thing, nevertheless, is certain: Jayas, the town, gave him some unique, unforgettable, even life-defining experiences; he credits it as the place where he received his first vision or darshan.

Historians have reconstructed Jayasi's life from sufi tazkiras (descriptions), legends and various traditions and hints given by the poet himself. It emerges that his was not a 'happy' life. He suffered from smallpox in early childhood, which resulted in him losing his left eye and being permanently short of hearing in the left ear. He gives his physical condition a movingly poetic twist in the course of his narrative: 'Since my beloved looked at me and spoke to me on my right side, I myself gave up my left eye and ear.'

मुहमद बाईं दिसि तजी एक सरवन एक आँखि।
जब ते दाहिन होइ मिला बोलु पपीहा पाँखि॥ —367

There is a story about the great poet Surdas who was blind. He was granted eyesight briefly and saw Krishna and Radha. He requested them to make him blind again as he did not want his vision, purified by their darshan, to be used for worldly affairs.

Jayasi also suffered great grief. He lost his parents when he was quite young, and later in life, he is believed to have lost his sons in an accident.

Jayasi was a Sufi of the Chishti Order, and has been described as an Indian researcher/seeker of Truth, a Muhaqqiq-i-Hind in the Sufi tazkiras. He was revered for having great spiritual achievements—barak—to his credit. In such contexts, achievements are articulated in the language of miracles. In popular memory, Jayasi too has his share of miracle-legends. One of these legends talks about his encounter with divinity due to his noble humanity.

Jayasi was too generous and social to eat alone. He had to have at least one fellow human being to share his Dastar-khwan i.e. dining table. One day a leper turned up exactly when Jayasi was about to take his meal. Jayasi invited him to join. Naturally, the leper was very hesitant, but Jayasi just would not listen. Very hesitantly, the leper joined Jayasi's Dastar-khwan. It so happened that when they were eating, some amount of pus from the leper's wounds dropped in the food, which was too little in any case to be thrown away. The leper offered to eat that portion, but Jayasi would not let him, and inspite of all the resistance from the leper, he proceeded to eat it—and lo and behold, the leper disappeared and a voice from the vacuum (Ghaibi Awaj) praised

Jayasi and conveyed Lord's appreciation of his noble humanity in action.

No wonder, such a noble man appreciated by Lord Himself, had the capacity to take any body-form at will and foresee future. He prophesied that he is destined to die 'by hunting'. The king of Jayas, who was a devoted admirer, made it known to everyone in his reign, that any hunter before going in for game, must ensure Jayasi's whereabouts. But, once a hunter came from outside the area, and as prophesied, Jayasi was 'hunted'; while roaming around in the form of a tiger.

Jayasi may or may not have met his end in such a miraculous and magical way, but the magic of his magnificent miracle—*Padmavat*—has continued to enchant the audience since the day it became known to the world. He had composed a couple of works before it as well but *Padmavat* is a stunning achievement and is considered the peak of the vernacular (mostly Awadhi) tradition of 'love-narratives' (prem-aakhayans*)*, coming down to Jayasi's times from the preceding two centuries.

Starting from Maulana Daud, the author of *Chandayan* (1370), the poets of these narratives merge features of two distinct literary traditions in their works. They follow the conventions of Persian masnavis—many of which, using the love-narratives as an allegory, are oriented towards explaining the teachings and practices of Sufi Islam. The Awadhi poets of love-narratives follow standard masnavi conventions. They begin their compositions with the praises of the Lord followed by eulogies of the Prophet of Islam, the early caliphs and the ruler of their own times (Shah-e-Waqt). Before embarking upon the story, the poets also introduce themselves. They follow the masnavi pattern in detailed, exaggerated description. They tell stories of their choice with various degrees of usage of conventions, forms and metaphors from not only Persian masnavis, but also from dastans (the tales orally performed for a group).

At the same time, the metres—doha and chaupai—and themes of these narratives are standard in the north Indian vernacular tradition. The theme of Maulana Daud's *Chandayan* is inspired by the folk tale about the love of Lorik and Chanda; other Sufi poets also follow the path shown by him. Today, the doha and chaupai forms are well-known through the *Ramcharitmanas* of Tulsidas, but the credit of first using them in epic compositions in Awadhi goes to these Sufi poets who borrowed not only the themes but also poetic forms, idioms, diction and metaphors etc. from everyday life, cultural memories, legends and mythologies of north India.

These poets were *not* writing the manuals of conversion to Islam. They were not 'strategically' choosing things 'alien' to them; these metres and folk tales came naturally to them. These stories belong to the Sufi poets as much as they do to Awadhi-speaking Hindus.

But let us also get rid of the tendency to assume that all Sufis were either equally liberal (since they practised yoga or talked of 'love') or propagandist (since 'they were only preaching Islam through their works'). Such simplistic generalizations are simply false. To know about each one of them individually is a must. Many Sufis practised yoga, spoke poetically of love, and at the same time, they were firm believers of Islam.

The famous Sheikh Farid of Ajodhan (Punjab) was a practitioner of yoga and some of his compositions, wherein he speaks passionately of 'love', are included in the holy book of the Sikh, the Adi Granth. But at the same time, he condemns as 'dogs' those who ignore the mandatory five-time namaz. He even recommends beheading of such deviant people (see Couplets 3 and 6 in *Sheikh Farid Ganj-e-Shakar*, in Hindi by Brajendra Kumar Singhal, Delhi, 2017).

Sheikh Abdu'l-Quddus of Gangoh (in Uttar Pradesh) composed *Alakh-Bani* in Hindi, elaborating the 'Sahaj Sabad Sadhna' (spontaneous practice of mysterious name) of Nathpanthi variety. He focused on the benefits of yogic practices for spiritual upliftment.

In this text, he comes across virtually as a Nathpanthi. But he also sent epistles to Babur recommending tax exemptions for Islamic scholars (ulemas) and Sufis, and at the same time, he advocated removal from important positions and other harsh measures against 'kafirs'—i.e. Hindus. (See the description of Sheikh Abdu'l-Quddus in *A History of Sufism in India* by S. A. A. Rizvi, Delhi, 1978.)

Jayasi was a Muslim, a Sufi in his belief, but Padmavat *is not a Sufi discourse or manual in the guise of an epic poem.*

Jayasi was an accomplished Sufi, but he was a poet, not a preacher. In *Padmavat*, he is not concerned with underlining the virtues of Islamic practices, even though he speaks vividly of his own faith through praises to Allah and the Prophet at the very beginning. In *Akharavat* (a work clearly aimed at articulating his own faith-system), he elaborates on Islamic beliefs using letters of the Nagri alphabet as springboards. Even here, his position is that of tolerance—respect for the followers of other faiths as well. He says of the Creator—'He fathered all the people and various lineages/ following their own faiths—Hindus and Muslims' (तिन्ह संतति उपराजा, भाँतिहि भाँति कुलीन/ हिन्दू तुरुक दुवौ भए, अपने अपने दीन).

Furthermore, he makes a remarkably 'Indian' truth-statement

on religious coexistence—'There are as many paths to God, as there are stars in the firmament, or pores in body; searching through any one of them a true seeker can find Him, feel satisfied and can sing his achievement...but well (so far as I am concerned), the way of Prophet Muhammad is the best and ought to be followed in the prescribed way including namaz, which in fact is the cornerstone of the faith' (विधना के मारग हैं ते ते। सरग नखत तन रोवाँ जेते। जेइ हेरा तेई तहँवे पावा। भा संतोष, समुझि मन गावा।...सो बड़ पंथ मुहम्मद केरा। है निरमल कबिलास बसेरा।...ना नमाज है दीन क थूनी। पढ़ैं नमाज सोई बड़ गूनी।).

Clearly, in order to understand our past and live out our present, we should listen to accomplished poets rather than religious preachers.

The tradition of love-narratives culminating in Jayasi's *Padmavat* reflects the excitingly creative outcome of the confluence of two cultures—first through aggression and resistance; and later on, through coexistence and interaction. The composers of these narratives wanted to write about the mysterious subtlety of human love and the ways of actualizing its inherent divinity. Naturally, not everyone was equally successful in articulating the divinity potential of love without slipping into traditional religiosity. Not everyone could create equally enchanting poetry either.

Jayasi is considered the best in this tradition because of the great poetic calibre and evocative ambiguity of *Padmavat*. Despite using esoteric terminology and metaphors liberally, *Padmavat* maintains emphasis on *human* love and its evocative power. Secondly, he creates the most beautiful tapestry of elements from Persian masnavi, dastan, Hindu epics and folklore.

More importantly, Jayasi, unlike his predecessors, takes a legend with a historical event as its background. Padmini of Chittor may or may not have been a historical figure but Alauddin certainly attacked Chittor in 1303 CE. Jayasi takes this event and transforms it into a remarkably moving tale of love, search, spiritual angst and sacrifice. He brilliantly merges fable, legend and fantasy with his chosen historical event. Unlike the court historians, Jayasi does not celebrate Alauddin's victory. Instead, he factually describes the capture of Chittor. In Jayasi's poetic reconstruction of the event, Alauddin the victor, instead of taking pride in his victory, regrets the destruction and reflects on the disastrous insatiability of uncontrolled desire. The crucial difference between a religious preacher, courtier and a poet is reiterated poignantly through this dramatic finale given by Jayasi to his epic.

The poet's sympathies are unambiguously with Padmavati and Ratansen—the tormented couple. In *Padmavat*, Ratansen is slain not in battle with Alauddin, but in a duel with fellow Rajput king, Devpal—who had lustful eyes for Padmavati. The fact that the king of Chittor was vanquished by Alauddin is thus given a twist, saving the hero from humiliation.

Jayasi employs popular memories, mythologies (both Hindu and Muslim) and legends to weave a tragic story of love and desire, death and destruction. Jayasi moves around with remarkable ease through both Hindu and Muslim traditions, and literary heritage. His knack for recognizing poetically poignant moments in the narrative and mastery over the craft of poetry is evident.

It is not surprising, therefore, that in the assessments of historians of Hindi literature, only Tulsidas's *Ramcharitmanas* (1574) surpasses *Padmavat* as an epic. It was composed in 1540, and its language, unlike that of *Ramcharitmanas*, is not overly Sanskritized and retains the local flavour of Awadhi. However, this makes comprehending *Padmavat* difficult for people outside Awadh. In addition to the problem, many words and expressions used by Jayasi have now become archaic.

The manuscripts of this Awadhi epic were mostly found written in Persian script. Acharya Ramchandra Shukla, the most influential historian of Hindi literature and a devoted Jayasi scholar, informs us that, '*Padmavat* was revered by Sufis as well as ordinary Muslims as a poem with "hidden mystic" meanings; most of its manuscripts were found in Muslim households.' He recalls from his 'personal experience' that 'such householders were found very liberal in outlook and reconciliatory by temperament.' Hopefully, this quality of *Padmavat* worked with Hindu households as well in Shukla's times. More urgently, let us hope, reading *Padmavat* will help generate a liberal outlook and reconciliatory temperament in our times.

None of the manuscripts, however, can be claimed to be in Jayasi's own handwriting. The sheer number and spread of the manuscripts indicate that *Padmavat* was an instant hit in literary circles and beyond. It was translated in Bengali within a hundred years of its composition.

Thus, the credit goes to Malik Muhammad Jayasi—a devout Muslim, a knowledgeable 'Indian seeker of Truth' writing in Awadhi—for taking the Padmavati legend of Rajasthan to Bengal; wherefrom a number of novels, plays and poems glorifying the Rajputs were to emanate in the nineteenth century.

The memory of the 'first garden'

The pain of his physical deformities, ugliness and consequent ridicule never left Jayasi, added to which there was the pain of significant emotional loss as well. In his *Aakhiri Kalaam* (The Final Statement) composed in 1529—a description of the 'day of the judgement' according to Islamic belief—Jayasi provides hints about his experience in Jayas. In its tenth stanza, he says:

> *I belong to Jayas, the town known as the first garden (Adi-Udyanu). I had come here as a guest only for a couple of weeks, and in this short duration passed through an experience, which gave me immense pleasure and turned me away from the world; and now recalling it gives me equally immense pain. It was an experience without which life was as good as death. That beauty permeated my vision and my heart. Wherever I saw, I saw only her/him, and nobody else. I just beheld the beauty and held the experience to myself; there was no 'other' person left; so with whom could I share it? I felt the whole world was a mirror reflecting my own self everywhere. That resplendent person had spread out the market (of beauty, grace?) in her/his playful manner; Malik Muhammad just passed through it one day, and was enchanted.*

(जायस नगर मोर अस्थानू। नगर क नाँव आदि उदयानू॥
तहाँ दिवस दस पहुने आएउँ। भा बैराग बहुत सुख पाएउँ॥
सुख भा सोचि एक दुख मानौ। ओहि बिनु जिवन मरन कै जानौ॥
नैन रूप सो गएउ समाई। रहा पूरि भर हिरदय छाई॥
जहँवें देखौ तहँवै सोई। और न आव दिस्टि तर कोई॥
आपुन देखि देखि मन राखौं । दूसर नाहि सो कासो भाखौं॥

सबै जगत दरपन के लेखा। आपन दरसन आपुहि देखा॥
अपने कौतुक कारन, मीर पसारिन हाट।
मलिक मुहम्मद बिहनै, होइ निकसिन तेहि बाट॥)

In Islamic as well as Hindu belief systems, paradise is identified as a garden of delights—Bagh-e-Rizwan in Islam and Nandan-Kanan in Hinduism. These are the 'first gardens' in religious imagination. What kind of experience prompted the poet to describe Jayas in terms evocative of the mythological memories rooted in this imagination?

Jayasi, being a great poet, was extremely conscious of the traditionally evolved connotation of each and every word; he chose his words carefully and with purpose. That is why his work is both a 'garden of delights' as well as a terrain of challenges for sensitive readers and scholars.

Jayas—an ordinary town for others is described as the 'first garden—a garden of delights' by Jayasi. He came there 'as a guest only for a couple of weeks', but then became one with it, became a part of it, became *Jayasi*. Why?

Because this town gave him an experience of great poignancy and magnitude which permeated his entire being; it turned the whole world into a mirror of his own self. It also left memories that were as immensely painful as the experience was pleasant. And all this was the result of a chance encounter, as indicated by the metaphor of 'one day passing through the market' of grace and beauty.

It seems this pain and pleasure, togetherness and separation were caused by engaging, bewitching and unfulfilled love. Such tragic love leads a man or woman to a state of bairag i.e. indifference to the world around. Love engulfs the lover and beloved in a parallel world of its own. Separation in such profound love leads to equally strong emotions. In some cases, suffering a tragedy may cause self-destruction; while in others, it may lead to transformation through an aesthetic or spiritual practice.

In Jayasi's case, as in the case with many others, the tragedy of separation might have been caused by natural or social reasons, or by misunderstanding; or even because of feeling discarded after being 'used'. Perhaps the poet mistook the appreciation of his poetry for affection and 'love'. There is a possibility that the misunderstanding led to some bitter exchanges. It is also likely that the moment of separation was further marred by sarcastic jibes at Jayasi's appearance and misfortune.

He intended to visit only for a brief while, but apparently stayed on in Jayas. He composed some parts of his epic (perhaps while still undergoing the experience of being in the 'garden of delights') during his stay. But then he left, probably dejected; and came back later in a pensive, reflective mood. After all, everyone

nurtures a longing of coming back at least once in life to his/her own 'garden of delights'. And, sometimes, one laments leaving it in the first place.

It happened with Kabir, who left Benares saying, 'What is the point of being a bhakta, if one has to die in Benares in order to reach the heavens.' 'The credit of having led a satisfactorily pure life belongs to Ram, not to Benares,' declared Kabir. But Benares was not merely a holy city as far as Kabir was concerned. For him, it was the city of his childhood and youth, friends and foes. Having left Benares for Maghar, Kabir regretted his decision, even condemning—quite uncharacteristically—his bhakti as 'shallow', as he had committed the 'blunder' of equating Benares with Maghar. (कासी मगहर सम बीचारी। ओछी भगति कैसे उतरसि पारी।)

Benares—the city of Kabir's childhood was (and is) a holy city for millions. Jayas—the city of Jayasi's first darshan—was his own 'first garden'. Although Kabir could not come back to the city of his childhood, Jayasi came back to his 'first garden' and completed his magnum opus *Padmavat* in 947 Hijri, that is, 1540 CE.

Jayasi's loaded references to his days in Jayas—the first garden—have been commented upon by scholars. The eminent Indologist Vasudeva Sharan Agrawal was the first to hint at some experience of this 'worldly' love. Later on, the poet-critic Vijay Dev Narayan Sahi developed this hint into a bold speculation about possible events that may have transpired: from rapture and affliction to infatuation and bitter separation—even scandal.

There are ample hints to support the above narration; but admittedly, no 'hard' evidence exists. The entire event or some parts of it may or may not have happened. We really don't know.

But one thing we know for sure, Malik Muhammad did not choose self-destruction. He took the path of transcending negative emotions like anger and frustration through creativity. He left Jayas physically, but in his mind and in his memories, he never left Jayas and Jayas never left him.

Malik Muhammad became *Jayasi* forever.

Love turns humans into the divine

Of course, the puritan mind can reduce the emotion underlying Jayasi's *Padmavat* to 'pure and harmless' spiritual love, and his epic to its allegory. The fact, however, remains that throughout the world the so-called 'mystic' poetry is rooted in and is evocative of the *human* emotion of love. In Indian tradition, desire (kama)—including the erotic kind—far from being seen as impure, has been venerated as an integral part of the four-fold ideal of life. In Bhakti and Sufi sensibilities, the element of eroticism is considered not only acceptable, but helpful, provided you have the competence to do the sadhana—observe the necessary steadfastness and profundity.

As mentioned above, in Jayasi's *Padmavat* the Awadhi tradition of love-narratives touched its peak; but such love-narratives were not confined to vernaculars only. Hasan Dilhawi (1253–1337), a contemporary of Amir Khusro, composed a masnavi called *Ishqnama* about the love between a Muslim boy and a Hindu girl of Nagore in Rajasthan, which ends in tragedy when the boy—not the girl—commits sati at the pyre of his beloved. Incidentally, in Jayasi's *Padmavat* too, Ratansen—the hero—when unable to meet Padmavati, tries to commit sati in desperation and is saved in the nick of time by Shiva and Parvati at Hanuman's request.

Hasan Dilhawi's work is based on an afsana (tale) that was popular at the time and he took it up because of its potential of conveying the force of 'true love' (ishq-i-haqiqi). Pranav Prakash, researcher at University of Iowa, is working on Hasan Dilhawi; I am grateful to him and Prof. Philip Lutgendroff for this information. Surely, more such works will come to light with further research.

On the other hand, bhakti, in the beginning, simply meant love, affection and sharing. Panini, the first grammarian of the world, defines it as such in his *Ashtadhayayi* (simply a 'work divided in eight chapters', composed four centuries before the Common Era). According to him, you can be a bhakta of Vasudev as well as of Mathura; the important point is the love and affection you feel for some god, place or human being. This sense of the word 'bhakta' can be seen even today in expressions like 'desh-bhakta' (a patriot).

Yaska (fifth century BCE), in his explanation of Vedic names and terms, describes Indra, Agni and Varun as 'bhaktas' of each other as they are companions and share things with each other. Gradually, the term 'bhakti' came to specifically signify 'devotion', even submission, to some god or goddess. But, even in this context, the bhakti-sutras of Narada (a text composed in the eleventh century by a sensitive soul who in a movingly self-effacing gesture attributed the text to that mythological archetype of bhakti—Narada) proclaim that the best way to do bhakti is to follow the example of the 'cowherd girls of Braj region' (यथा व्रजगोपिकानाम्). The Gopikas did not have a relation of meek and torrid surrender with Krishna. Theirs was a relationship of sharing on an equal footing, of playful companionship in love—characterized by pleasure, love-sport and the pain of separation.

A century before Jayasi, Kabir had unambiguously announced his faith in the continuum of erotic and spiritual. He clearly stated that the erotic, when understood properly and sensitively, leads to the spiritual. Everyone has the hidden, unrealized potential of this transformative experience. In order to counter the simplistic, insensitive puritanism, which in his times donned the garb of 'revered traditional values' (just as it does in our times), Kabir took care to refer to the authority of the Shrimad Bhagvata.

Profoundly understood and practised, the erotic desire
Can take you to Ram
What can poor Kabir say,
When Shukadeva testifies the same.

(काम मिलावे राम कूं जो कोई जाने साध
कबीर बिचारा क्या करे, सुखदेव बोले साख)

—Kabir Granthavali, Sadh Sakhibhut ko ang, 11

Shukadeva, as we know, was the son of Vedavyasa and had narrated the Shrimad Bhagvata—essentially the story of Krishna's love and life—to King Parikshit. Kabir never composed an epic of love but he was not merely a poet of social criticism. In fact, his poetic sensibility is essentially of love and his most moving poems revolve around the theme of love. When he poetically reconstructs and reflects on various moments and shades of love, he almost always puts on a feminine persona and speaks as if a woman in love is speaking. But in his didactic moments, he sounds quite misogynistic. A misogynist while discoursing on existential illusions known as 'maya' and a woman while speaking of love—this is the main paradox of Kabir's poetic sensibility.

Jayasi's *Padmavat* does not carry this paradox. This epic is Jayasi's creative and reflective ode to the memories of pleasure and pain he came across during his life in Jayas—the 'first garden'. Despite these painful memories, he is never seen slipping into misogynistic outbursts. The only exception is Ratansen scolding his first wife, Nagmati, in a typically male chauvinistic idiom. But that is the king talking, not the poet. As mentioned earlier, just like Kabir, Jayasi too borrowed many idioms and imagery from the Nathpanthi stock, but he chose to compose his epic in the tradition of love-narratives. Many of these narratives were Sufi, but there were others which were neither Sufi nor Bhakti in their orientation. We will briefly refer to one such 'secular' love-narrative in our discussion. This tradition of love-narratives by its very nature excluded the possibility of the fair sex being seen as a personification of maya; as an impediment to pursuits of higher truths.

Many people have many kinds of experiences, but only those who reconstruct such experiences in a layered texture become great poets. Jayasi was one such poet; reading *Padmavat* is indeed like walking through a 'garden of delight'—Nandan-Kanan or Bagh-e-Rizwan. His descriptions of feminine beauty and lovemaking eliminate the difference between the carnal and transcendental, erotic and sublime.

Jayasi unambiguously declares his belief in the power of love—'human beings becoming divine through love', or 'human love has reached a divine status'—when he says, *Manush Prem Bhayau Baikunthi* (मानुष प्रेम भयउ बैकुंठी।).

The discrete subtlety of references to the impact of days spent in the 'first garden' stands in sharp contrast to anguished, explicit references to Jayasi's deformities and 'ugly' appearance. The poet himself makes it loud and clear in his work. Along with this consciousness of 'ugliness', unlike many Bhakti and Sufi poets, Jayasi was most insistent on his poetic persona. He confronted his bodily deformities, ugly appearance and the insensitive ridicule through his brilliant wit and justly unshakable confidence in the power of his poetry. In one of the legends, Jayasi shames the king who is laughing at his ugliness with the question—'You are laughing at me or at the potter?'—an anguished and witty reference to the One who has made all of us. In some versions of this legend, the 'king' who was left embarrassed and apologetic was none other than Sher Shah Suri himself.

The tale of Padmavati as told by Jayasi is covered at both the ends with his anguish at his physical deformities and 'ugly' appearance. Following the pattern of Persian masnavis, he starts with detailed praises to God, His Prophet and His companions, proceeds to praise the ruler at the time (Shah-e-Waqt), Sher Shah Suri, and expresses his admiration and gratitude to his own guru, Sheikh Mahdi. Finally, the poet comes to himself and the first sentence of self-description reads:

Though single-eyed, Muhammad is a meritorious poet,
anyone listening to his poetry is enchanted.

(एक नैन कवि मुहम्मद गुनी
सोइ विमोहा जेइँ कवि सुनी)

He fought the fallout of his bodily deformities through his epic creation and tried to transform the traumatic experience of losing his love into an aesthetic experience. It is not for nothing that Jayasi described his *Padmavat* as a text 'written in his own blood and tears'.

It is remarkable that in the entire epic, no one is ridiculed on account of any kind of physical handicap or 'ugliness'. Neither the poet nor any of his characters indulge in 'poking fun' of anyone's appearance.

Padmavat, *amongst other things, is also a powerful antidote to the disease of body shaming.*

Padmini before *Padmavat*

By the fifteenth century, the legend of Padmini of Chittor had been in circulation for some time and was known widely enough for the poet Malik Muhammad to have heard it in Jayas—the small town in Awadh where he was based. Alauddin Khalji had attacked and captured Chittor more than two centuries before the composition of *Padmavat.* Khusro—the famous poet, Sufi and a courtier of Alauddin—accompanied Khalji and does not mention Padmini in his account. Later chronicles also don't mention her. In fact, very little historical details about the siege and battle of Chittor and its aftermath, and its ruler Ratan Singh (not Ratansen according to the chronicles), are available.

But Padmini was 'present' in the oral traditions and legends of Rajasthan, which attracted Jayasi. Interestingly, however, these legends and traditions were written down only *after* Jayasi's *Padmavat.* There are two well-known written versions of the

Padmini legend. The first is by Hemratan (1588 CE) and the second by Jatmal Nahar (1627 CE). Both narrate the story along similar lines—Ratansen going to Simhal in order to get Padmini, Raghav Chetan provoking Alauddin, the siege of Chittor, capture of Ratansen by deceit, and his liberation due to cleverness and bravery of the warrior Gora and his young nephew Badal. Recently, another version, not much different from the aforementioned two, has been published by Sh. Brajendra Kumar Simhal (*Rani Padmini*, New Delhi: Vani Prakashan, 2017).

Both Hemratan and Jatmal focus on the intelligence, bravery, war skills and 'word of honour' (given to Padmavati) of the warriors—Gora and Badal. The works of both these authors are titled as such—the saga of Gora and Badal. Hemratan's composition is known as *Gora Badal ri Chupai* and Jatmal's as *Gora Badal ri Baat* (or *Katha*). The real hero of both these accounts is the warrior Gora, who dies in battle and whose wife commits sati. Both Gora and the victorious survivor, Badal, are blessed by the grateful couple—Padmini and Ratansen.

In Hemratan's account, Ratansen complains about the quality of food, to which his first wife, Prabhavati (who was proud of her expertise in seventy cuisines), irritably responds by challenging him to find a woman of his choice; one who would serve him better food, a 'padmini' of Simhal. Ratansen leaves vowing that he will only take food after he has found a 'padmini [woman]'. In folk tradition, young princes and men often left in this manner in search of a 'padmini'.

In Jatmal's account, a bard comes to the court of Ratansen and sings the praises of the resplendent beauty of padminis (the word padmini is used generically here) of Simhal. The king's desire is fired. At this moment, a yogi appears in the court. The king seeks his help, the yogi is only too willing, and the king leaves with him on his mission.

It is interesting that both these accounts, and others written in the following years, end on an overall happy note. Ratansen is released from captivity; Alauddin's designs are defeated. On the other hand, Jayasi's telling of the story, as is well-known, ends in a tragedy of sublime dimensions.

Chhitai Charit

The only written, pre-Jayasi reference to Padmini of Chittor and Alauddin's obsession with her is found in a literary romance called *Chhitai Charit*, composed between 1475 and 1480 CE in Gwalior. This text was begun by Narayan Das and completed by Ratanrang and Devchandra. These poets were patronized by the Tomar kings of Gwalior.

Chhitai Charit is unique amongst such texts from the period; it is clearly a 'secular' romance in the sense that its poetic intent does not have a Sufi or Bhakti inclination, nor has there been any such religious or 'spiritual' subtext attributed to it by the audience.

The term 'Charit' means story, and *Chhitai Charit* tells the story of Chhitai, the daughter of Devgiri's King Ramdev. She was married to Samar Singh, prince of Dwarsamudra, who was an accomplished veena player. Importantly, in this text, the relationship between Ramdev and Alauddin passes through the ups and downs of friendship and confrontation. To cut a long story short, Alauddin gets fascinated by Chhitai and wants to possess her. While expressing his obsession to his adviser, Raghav Chetan, he says, 'I attacked Ranthambore for Deval Devi, but was unsuccessful. Then I heard of Padmini of Chittor and imprisoned Ratansen, but Badal freed him. Now, if I don't get Chhitai, I will just commit suicide.'

It is not clear, whether the word 'padmini' here is being used by Alauddin as a proper noun, as a name of a particular person, or as a generic term referring to an exceptionally beautiful woman.

Whatever be the case, the author(s) of this romance give a very interesting twist to the tale at the moment of Chhitai's abduction by Alauddin. She tells him, 'You have been friends with my father and I have always seen you as a father figure. I expect you to reciprocate the sentiment with respect and fatherly affection' (तबहि छिताई जानिउं साहा। अब मो वचन एक निरबाहा॥ पाप दिष्ट जन चितवहिं मोही। पिता बराबर जानउं तोही॥). Alauddin is flustered, nevertheless, he promises to indeed treat Chhitai as a daughter (अब मो तूं कन्या वरु जाना). Chhitai lives under Alauddin's protection, in the house of Raghav Chetan who, unlike in Jayasi's *Padmavat*, is not a crafty and villainous character in this story. Samar Singh, Chhitai's husband, reaches the royal court as a veena-playing yogi, and is recognized by Chhitai, who then informs Alauddin. He gives the couple a loving and respectful farewell, with valuable ornaments as parting gifts, standing by his word to act like a father towards Chhitai (पिता सबदु तइं बोलउं मोही। बेटी वरु जानौं हउ तोही॥...दीए साहि आभरन गढ़ाई। हीरा रंगु सरंग जराई॥... अब घर कुशल आपने जाही। दई विदा यौं बोलइ साही॥...)

This detour into *Chhitai Charit* was important not only to trace the pre-Jayasi literary reference to 'Padmini of Chittor', but also to get a sense of the literary culture of those times. Many of us impose the present issues on, and seek their solutions from the past, thus violating the pastness of the past and harming both our present and future. In *Chhitai Charit*—a work composed by Hindu poets in the court of a Hindu king in the fourteenth century—we get a glimpse of the complexity of that era, the richness of its literary culture and poetic imagination. The work describes the intricate human emotions and treats poignant situations in a humane and sensitive manner. It refrains from reducing the characters into good guys and bad guys on the basis of their religion. This indicates the perspective of the three poets, and tells us something about the evolving mindset in that early modern era of Indian history.

Chhitai Charit's treatment of Alauddin is revealing and thought-provoking. The poet(s) had no reason to please Alauddin (deceased more than a century ago), not even his descendants, as they served not the Muslim court of Delhi, but a Hindu one at Gwalior.

Padmavat also refers to Chhitai, but in a very general way, and in consonance with Alauddin's personality as conceived by Jayasi. Sarja—the messenger sent by Alauddin to Ratansen—simply says, 'It is futile for you to think of facing the Sultan's onslaught; come what may, he will have his way, just as he wanted Chhitai and got her.' No trace here (in the work of a Muslim poet) of the noble, fatherly touch given to Alauddin's character by the Hindu poets of *Chhitai Charit*.

A poet rooted in his times

Jayasi was a practising Sufi and composed *Aakhiri Kalaam* in accordance with Islamic theology, but that is not the case with his other works. In fact, in *Kanhavat*, he retells the story of Krishna as found in the Bhagvata. As far as *Padmavat* is concerned, if at all he wanted to preach anything here, it was spirituality beyond any religious denomination. Far from being opposed to the erotic aspect of human nature, this spirituality is actualized through human, carnal love which in its depth becomes sublime and transforms mortal humans into immortal and divine.

Yes, *Padmavat*'s poetic idiom has elements of Sufism, but then it also has the elements from the Nath tradition and Hindu mythology. The historical event of Alauddin attacking Chittor forms the backdrop of the tale told by Jayasi. His hero Ratansen goes to Simhal (a uniquely Indian motif) island in the guise of a Nathpanthi yogi, not as a Sufi fakir. His companions are also yogis, not Muslim fakirs. The poet's acquaintance with Hindu traditions and his roots in everyday life of Awadh determine the choice of his idioms, metaphors and allusions. His knowledge, and organic connect with Hindu traditions and idioms is so spontaneous, deep and rich that it can intimidate many Hindus, including self-appointed guardians of Hinduism.

Possessing an excellent sense of the poignancy of cultural memories, Jayasi describes the final departure of Ratansen and Padmavati as the 'disappearance of Ram and Sita' (भए अलोप राम और सीता). At the end of the Ram Katha, only Sita had 'disappeared', as she was banished. Here, both 'Ram' and 'Sita' disappear.

Ramcharitmanas was yet to be composed, but obviously, Ram Katha was deeply rooted in the popular memory. Its episodes

and characters contributed significantly (as they still do) to the everyday speech of people. Being a 'son of the soil' of Awadh, Jayasi's fascination with Ram Katha was very natural. This interest led to so many allusions and references to Ram Katha that, Vasudeva Sharan Agrawal in his illuminating commentary on *Padmavat* says, 'A little Jayasi-Ramayan can be carved out of the *Padmavat*.'

Given his vast knowledge and experience, incidences, stories and motifs not only from Ram Katha, Mahabharata and the Puranas but also from the Nathpanthi tradition and Islamic theology came naturally to Jayasi. The same is the case with popular wisdom, folk tales and folk motifs. He possessed a great treasure in the form of systematic knowledge, popular wisdom and cultural memories and had the genius of merging them together very effectively. In *Akharavat*, he uses the name 'Narada' in such a way that it brings to mind both Narada Muni of Hindu tradition and Iblis of Islamic one. Iblis was the most dedicated devotee of God, but rebelled due to the primacy God had given to Adam. The most important (and most ironical according to Islamic, particularly Sufi belief) fact, however, remains that Iblis was the most loving devotee or bhakta of God. That is why he resented Adam. After he was condemned and banished by God, he deceived human beings and 'whispered' in their ears to take them away from God's way.

Narada Muni in Hindu tradition is a great devotee and has moments of irritation with his Narayan (Vishnu) whose name he otherwise utters constantly. He is taught a lesson or two by Narayan when he thinks too much of himself; but never faces expulsion from Vaikunth. In any case, he hardly stays there. Narada is prone to constant wandering and 'breaking news', often with some added mischief. The fact remains, however, that he is one of the archetypes of devotion—bhakti. As I mentioned earlier, the most important and influential theoretical expositions of bhakti—the concise sutras—have been attributed to Narada.

Keeping all this in mind, it is striking to hear what Jayasi says at one place in *Akharavat*, 'Narada laments the fact that he has been defeated by a weaver' (ना नारद रोइ रोइ पुकारा/ एक जुलाहे सों मैं हारा).

This line has been interpreted as a glowing tribute from Jayasi to the great bhakta and weaver from Benares—Kabir, who had passed away in 1518, only two decades before Jayasi completed his *Padmavat*.

Akharavat was not intended to be an epic—it is not even great poetry—whereas *Padmavat* was composed consciously as an epic of human love and it overflows with the illuminating treasures of knowledge, wisdom and cultural memories. Jayasi has turned his 'inner journey' of coming to terms with the memories of the 'first darshan in the first garden' into a literary masterpiece.

It does not, however, mean that *Padmavat* was not read, revered or used by Sufis. It most definitely was, but that is a different matter altogether. No poet—Jayasi, Tulsidas, Kabir or Mira—can control the use of his/her work, but such use should not be confused with poetic intent. *Padmavat* was certainly popular amongst Sufis, but not *only* amongst them.

As indicated already, *Padmavat* was an instant hit in its own times. In the modern times, ever since the most influential historian of Hindi literature, Ramchandra Shukla published his edition of *Padmawat* (1924), its excerpts have inevitably been included in Hindi syllabi, from school to postgraduate programmes. In the very beginning of his introduction, Shukla situated the text in a historical context, wherein after initial conflicts, Hindus and Muslims were coming to terms with each other:

'A century ago, Kabir had already castigated bigotry of every kind. One is not sure of the pundits and mullahs, but ordinary people had recognized the unity of Ram and Rahim...only those sadhus and fakirs could hope to win the popular admiration who seemed beyond differentiating on the religious lines... For Hindus and Muslims both, it was time for opening up to each other. People were tending towards sharing instead of distancing. Muslims were willing to listen to the Rama-story of Hindus and Hindus were ready to hear the dastan of Hamja...and sometimes both even tried to explore the pathways to God together.'

To Shukla, *Padmavat* was a luminous signpost of this shared search for the pathway to God. He wrote about *Padmavat* with as great a passion and critical acumen as he wrote about his favourite poet—Tulsidas. Taking his cue from the 'first of the last stanzas' of the epic, which supposedly 'provides the key' to Sufi content 'hidden' in the text, Shukla concludes that it is an allegory to the

Sufi spiritual practice. But, Mata Prasad Gupta—the great text-critic and scholar of early modern vernacular literature of north India—in his edition of *Padmavat* (1952) based on a comparative study of sixteen manuscripts from different periods, comes to the far more convincing conclusion that the so-called 'key-providing' stanza was 'added to the text much later'.

Jayasi faithfully follows the poetic and Puranic tradition of indicating a Phalashruti. The Phalashrutis as a rule foretell the material and spiritual benefits accruing to the audience. The Rajasthani poet Jatmal who was neither a bhakta nor a Sufi, at the end of his *Gora Badal ri Baat,* makes this Phalashruti—'One who listens to this katha, will get all the worldly riches (nav-nidhi*)* and will lead a life free of all obstacles.'

No such luck for *Padmavat*'s reader. S/he is only promised an enhancement of sensitivity and a transfer of capacity for 'singing of love—Muhammad has composed this poem in blood and tears. One who listens to it will himself/herself be able to sing the torments of love':

(मुहम्मद यहि कवि जोर सुनावा। सुना जो पेम पीर गा पावा॥
जोरी लाइ रकत कै लेई। गाढ़ी प्रीति नैन जल सोई॥)

Reading Jayasi's *Padmavat* is not going to make you rich or famous overnight. Its only hope is to make you more sensitive to people and creatures around you. Jayasi's '*Manush Prem Bhayau Baikunthi*' is not a promise of providing easy passage to the paradise of any religion. Jayasi only says that if you live love in its totality, you will have the deepest spiritual and creative experience. In other words, you will come to know Vaikunth within your heart.

Jayasi, the Sufi, had achieved a certain level of karamaat—the capacity to perform miracles. But Jayasi, the poet of *Padmavat*, did not expect anything 'other-worldly' or 'miraculous' from his epic, except for being remembered as the one who told this tale of love:

Who in this world does not long for abiding fame?
I hope, the readers of this story will also remember my name.

(केइँ न जगत जस बेंचा केइँ न लीन्ह जस मोल।
जो यह पढ़ै कहानी हम सँवरै दुइ बोल॥)

His hope was indeed vindicated. Almost five centuries after his death, Jayasi continues to be remembered with admiration and gratitude. A sensitive reader of *Padmavat* finds Jayasi's Phalashruti coming true; s/he feels the transfer of capacity of singing of love at least in the form of appreciation. Acharya Shukla did well in starting his introduction to *Padmawat* with the condemnation of bigotry. Generally speaking, the capacity to appreciate good poetry does not sit easily with bigotry of any kind.

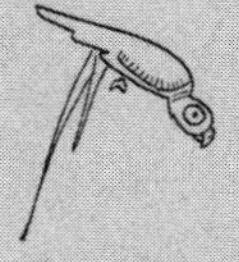

Chapter 1

The Simhal Princess and Her Parrot

A twilight zone of history and fantasy

Now, we are ready to have a sense of Jayasi's epic, to 'listen' to his reconstruction of the tale he had 'heard' and chose to turn into an exploration of erotic desire.

Before embarking on this journey, let us be clear, that Jayasi was neither writing history, nor simply recording the story, as he 'heard' it. He was employing what Sanskrit poetic calls, 'Gadharudha Pratyaya' (a theme well-entrenched in popular memory) to articulate his reflections on the vagaries of love and life in general. Jayasi had to make his basic statement—*love turns humans into the divine*—through an epic structure; he needed a motif and theme, which was well-known, but not already recognized as divine. What would be the point to say 'love turns humans into

divine' with reference to a story that was recognized as divine anyway? How would the idea of erotic-spiritual continuum and the process of transformation be conveyed through such an already revered story?

Our poet was not looking for such divine stories; he also did not intend to portray his hero and heroine as some kind of incarnations or deities. His Padmavati is more than extraordinary. Her beauty is a living reminder of the grace of God and the perfection of His creation. Even so, she is not a devi but rather a woman of this very world—extremely attractive, erotically competent, devoted as a wife and intelligent and courageous enough to negotiate a difficult situation. And yet, 'ordinary' enough to enter into a jealous verbal duel and even a fist fight with the 'other woman' (i.e. Nagmati—Ratansen's first wife) in her man's life.

Jayasi needed a 'well-known' story, but a story too well-known for its details wouldn't serve his purpose either. He needed a story with some built-in ambiguity; a story which would serve as a departure point for his journey into a creative recollection of his own experience, and reflections on love and desire in general.

He chose the story of Padmini from the oral traditions of Rajputana, but shifted its emphasis crucially. He did not write a saga of bravery and honour of Gora and Badal, but the narratives of love between Padmavati and Ratansen, friendship of Padmavati and Hiraman—her parrot, and the silent sufferings of Nagmati.

Given his poignant and convincing storytelling on one hand and historicity of Alauddin's siege and capture of Chittor on the other, Jayasi's epic has turned Padmini of Chittor into an important figure in popular memory. Padmini's historicity continues to be a matter of debate amongst historians, but the gadharudha (entrenched in popular memory) status of her story was indisputably fortified after the composition of Jayasi's *Padmavat.*

Generally, popular memory turns historical events into legends; Jayasi's genius has turned the legend of Padmini into 'real history'; in fact she has become more than real—irrespective of her historicity. His creative genius created not only a poetic work of historic importance, but history itself.

Where is Simhal?

There has been a lot of speculation about the identity of Simhal island mentioned in Jayasi's *Padmavat.* Many historians have 'located' it within Rajasthan. However, a careful reading of *Padmavat* reveals that even if Simhal is not an actual place but the poet's representation of a fabulous utopia, one can 'reach' Simhal by passing through real geographical locations, which Jayasi accurately describes.

Hiraman, Padmini's parrot, guides Ratansen to Simhal, laying down the route diligently and promptly; he makes clear at the outset that 'at a certain point, *one way will take you towards Simhal and the other to Lanka;* it is important to know the difference for which you need a really knowledgeable guide'. Hiraman further adds, 'Only he who has seen the path himself can be a proper guide. How can one without wings even imagine taking flight?

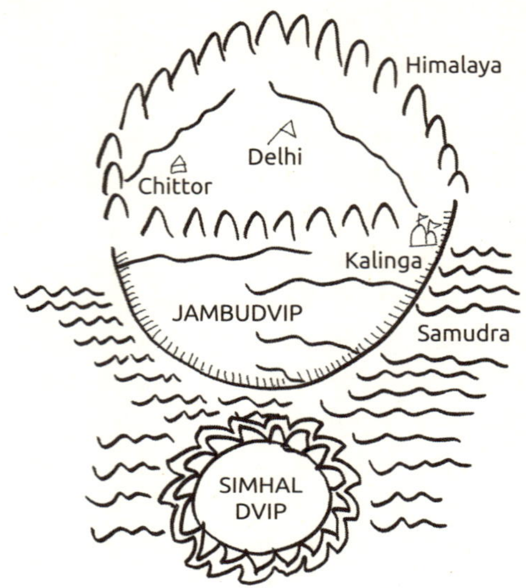

Such a guide would only be like a branch that takes leaves along with it under water. Two blind men cannot help each other find the way. Listen carefully, king, if you want to take the right path. You should take the route via Bijanagar, don't go towards Kunda and Gola; also avoid Andhiyar on your left. Stick to the correct path. Telangana will be on your right in the south and Gadha Katanga in north. When you reach Ratanpur, the hills of Jharkhand will be on your left.

Ratanpur is the gateway to Odisha, but that exactly is not your destination. From Ratanpur, you have to take the sea route towards its right.'

ततखन बोला सुआ सरेखा। अगुआ सोइ पंथ जेइँ देखा॥
सो का उड़ै न जेहि तन पाँखू। लै सो परासहिं बूड़ै साखू॥
जस अंधा अंधे कर संगी। पंथ न पाव होइ सइंलगी॥
सुनु मति काज चहसि सौं साजा। बीजानगर बिजैगिरि राजा॥
पूँछु न कहां कुंड और गोला। तजु बाँएँ अंधियार खटोला॥

दक्खिन दहिनै रहे तिलंगा। उत्तर माँझे गढ़ा खटंगा॥
माँझ रतनपुर सौंह दुआरा। झारखंड दे बाऊं पहारा॥
आगें पाऊं ओडैसा बाएँ देहु सो बाट।
दहिनावर्त लाई कै उत्तरु समुद्र के घाट॥ —138

This description of the route from Rajasthan to Odisha is perfectly accurate. Vijaypur is still a town in Malwa (Madhya Pradesh). From there, Ratansen is instructed not to move towards Gadha and Konda (i.e. southern tip of Chhattisgarh) and also to avoid present-day Sagar in Madhya Pradesh; he is told to proceed towards Ratanpur which lies between Telangana on the right and Jharkhand on the left. Ratanpur is near present-day Bilaspur and Jayasi is quite right in describing it as the gateway to Odisha—from where Ratansen has to take a sea route.

Ratansen is welcomed by the king of Odisha—Gajapati—who cautions Ratansen about the hazards of the voyage ahead of him. In response to his friend's advice, Ratansen emphasizes the totality of his love. 'I know all the hazards,' he says, 'but if one is really in love, how do the oceans matter? I am indifferent to the ocean or Ganga, and just look forward to Padmavati's grace whose beggar I am.'

While praising King Gajapati's commitment to friendship and his generosity, Jayasi mentions both Karna of the Mahabharata and Hatim of Islamic legends—'They knew the art of giving, that is why they are known as upholders of the dharma' (हातिम करन दिया जौं सिखा। दिया अहा धरमन्हि महँ लिखा).

King Gajapati realizes that Ratansen is not merely infatuated, but possessed by true love. Gajapati's realization is affirmed by the poet's own voice, 'Why expect too much from this life which is as transient as half a second's dream. Says Muhammad, the real sadhus are those who live in awareness of ever-present death, who spend their lives as if already dead':

> एहि जीवन के आस का जस सपना तिल आधु।
> मुहमद जिअतहि जे मरहिं तेइ पुरुष साधु॥ —146

Realizing the futility of any advice or caution to a 'man living as if already dead', Gajapati provides his friend with a fleet of his best ships and wishes Ratansen good luck on his journey.

From this point, the narration enters into the realm of fable and fantasy. The voyager now has to cross the seven seas starting with an ocean of water and then oceans of milk, curd and wine; coming to the most ferociously unfriendly one—the Kilkila sea—which can be crossed only by those who are truthful and courageous in their sadhana, devoted in their love and have the benefit of the guidance of a true guide—a real guru. Those who manage to cross it finally reach Mansar where in the glory of their success, they blossom like the lotus and radiate like the sun. And it is in this calm, serene sea that Simhal is located.

Just as Jayasi's description of the route to Simhal is geographically accurate, so is the veracity of the king of Odisha he mentions. The Gajapati dynasty ruled Odisha from 1435 to 1555 CE. It was during the reign of Gajapati King Kapilendra Deva (1435–1466) that Sarala Das, the Odia poet, wrote the Odia Mahabharata.

Throughout his epic, the poet moves with remarkable felicity from the realistic to fabulous; from historical to imaginary; from this world to the sublime. This felicity gives a unique richness to the texture of his epic and a multilayered poignancy to its structure. It is important to keep this crucial fact in mind and avoid the modern mistake of reading everything factually. The poet is of course aware of historical and geographical facts, but is writing an epic, not a chronicle. The location of Simhal hardly makes any difference to Jayasi's poetic purpose, nor should it affect our appreciation of his work.

Nevertheless, it is interesting to note that Simhal is located beyond Odisha, not in modern-day Rajasthan or Sri Lanka. In fact, Jayasi underlines its difference from Sri Lanka when he describes his Simhal in detail. Moreover, when Ratansen has reached Simhal but has not yet met Padmini, Hiraman describes him to the princess as having 'come form the western parts'. Had Simhal been identical with or close to Sri Lanka in Jayasi's imagination, Hiraman would describe Ratansen as someone from the north.

Incidentally, according to *Bisaldeva Raas*, a bardic poem composed in Rajasthan by Nalha, two centuries before Jayasi's *Padmavat,* another king—Bisaldeva of Ajmer—had travelled to Odisha, where 'diamonds were found as abundantly as was salt in his kingdom'.

Jayasi has created a twilight zone of history, legend and fantasy in which you can see and hear silhouettes of historical characters and locations working in tandem with the legendary ones. He merged and moulded the given narratives of Padmini of Simhal and Alauddin's siege of Chittor to put the sublimity of erotic in a perspective of transience of life. His focus is on love, beauty and their enchantment; and on the disaster caused by unjust desire.

Jayasi did not intend to either propagate Sufism or the valour and honour of any community. His epic extends an invitation to hear neither 'as it happened' kind of reportage, nor an 'inspiring' call to honour and valour; but to listen to a tale of love, its various dimensions and its vagaries written in a poet's 'blood and tears'.

Jayasi's Padmavat is an invitation to reflect on erotic desire and its elevation into an experience of 'divinity within'.

Beginning: The creator and his creation

Padmavat opens with praises to the Lord; these are the praises of an accomplished poet, not a mere believer. He goes on to describe the Lord's majesty and the magnificence of His creation in a series of striking metaphors along with allusions to Islamic and Hindu traditions. He refers to the prophet of Islam: 'God created a blemish-less man (कीन्हेसि पुरुष एक निरमरा), whose name was Muhammad, he was designated as teacher of humanity.'

But what acquires a very special, personal poignancy is this:

'He has given many gems, whose value slow-witted humans often don't recognize. He has given the palate and capacity to enjoy delicious delicacies. He has given teeth which give chuckling its attraction. He has given eyes to behold all of creation and ears to hear sounds and voices. He has given the tongue to speak, and palms and arms to act. He has given feet so that one can move. The value of all these limbs is truly appreciated only by someone who is deprived of any one of these. The value of youth is truly known only to the old who cannot go back to being young, howsoever desperately they long for it. The kings do not know the value of pleasure, it is known only to those who live in penury.

'The value of a healthy body is not known to those who are fit to enjoy it all, it is known only to those not keeping well. Of course, the One, who resides in every heart knows the essence of everything':

(अउर जो दीन्हेसि रतन अमोला। ताकर मरम न जानइ भोला॥
दीन्हेसि रसना ओ रस भोगू। दीन्हेसि दसन जो विहँसइ जोगू॥
दीन्हेसि जग देखइ कहँ नैना। दीन्हेसि स्रवन सुनइ कहँ बैना॥
दीन्हेसि कंठ बोल जेहिं माहाँ। दीन्हेसि कर पल्लौ बर बाँहा॥
दीन्हेसि चरन अनूप चलाहीं। सोई जान जेहिं दीन्हेसि नाहीं॥
जोबन मरम जान पै बूढ़ा। मिला न तरुनापा जब ढूँढ़ा॥
सुख कर मरम न जानइ राजा। दुखी जा जा कहँ दुख बाजा॥
काया क मरम जान पै रोगी भोगी रहइ निचिंत।
सब कर मरम गोसांई जानइ जो घट घट महँ नित॥) —9

Being able to see in only one eye, and hear in one ear, as well as his pockmarked face (due to smallpox) in early childhood, Jayasi knew the pain of suffering from bodily deformities and 'ugliness'. More importantly, he found a way out instead of succumbing to negativity. In the very next stanza, he talks about the unlimited treasure of positivity and other qualities possessed by the Lord, from which, He gives out generously to the deserving. No human achievement is possible without God's grace, human beings eager to credit themselves should know this. In fact:

God wants positive qualities to spread far and wide, He does it Himself and for this purpose also 'creates' positive and talented people—who act as instruments for spreading positive qualities and thinking all around.

(बड़ गुनवंत गोसांईं चहइ सो होइ तेहि बेगि।
औ अस गुनी संवारइ जो गुन करइ अनेग॥) —10

Being so gifted was divine compensation for all the physical deformities, ridicule, deprivations and deceits Jayasi suffered in his life. Yes, he suffered a loss of love, perhaps even a separation coloured with negativity, but why would he pity himself? Through his talent and competence, he overcame all the negativity, becoming a divine instrument of spreading positivity all around. Through the positive qualities (guna) he got as God's grace and blessing, he transformed his own pleasure and pain into everyone's garden of literary delights and challenges.

Padmavat works not only as an antidote to the disease of body shaming, but also as a cautionary tale against self-pity.

Ruby in the dust

Having praised God, the Prophet of Islam and his companions, and then the ruler of the times followed by his own spiritual preceptor—Sheikh Mahadi—Jayasi comes to himself before embarking upon the story of Padmini of Simhal.

Throughout *Padmavat*, the poet describes everything (from culinary feasts to horses) in great detail, in long shots as well as in close-ups, as if insistently saying that even if he has been deprived of sight in one eye, his 'eye for detail' and his 'vision'—in other words, his ability to put details in perspective—more than makes up for his physical handicap.

The poet goes on to compare himself with other great 'achievers' who with their deformities have made a unique place for themselves in the universe. In this stanza, the audience also gets an early hint of his vast knowledge of systematic, academic knowledge (Shastras) as well as folk wisdom: '[The] moon has been created by the Creator with its spots,' says the poet, 'and it gives pleasing light to the world.'

Further, he says, 'So what, if I am one-eyed? There is after all only one brightest star—Venus—in the firmament. How can you expect fragrance in the mango unless you accept the sharpness and stickiness of its stem ends? Ocean water is salty, because its spread is limitless beyond comprehension. Mount Sumeru was hit by Lord Shiva's trident before it turned golden and touched the sky. Unless passed through fire, gold is not purified.'

Jayasi concludes with words of supreme self-confidence:

'The poet's single eye is like a mirror and his poetic emotion is free of any ill will, all the beautiful and handsome ones fall at his feet and look forward to words emanating from his mouth.'

एक नैन कवि मुहमद गुनी। सोई विमोहा जेइँ कवि सुनी॥
चाँद जइस जग विधि औतारा। दीन्ह कलंक कीन्ह उजिआरा॥
जग सूझा एकइ नैनाहाँ। उवा सूक अस नखतन्ह माहाँ॥
जौं लहि अंबहि डाभ न होई। तौ लगि सुगंध बसाइ न सोई॥
कीन्ह समुद्र पानि जौ खारा। तौ अति भएउ असूझ अपारा॥
जौं सुमेरु तिरसूल बिनासा। भा कंचनगिरि लाग अकासा॥
जौं लहि घरी कलंक न परा। काँच होइ नहिं कंचन करा॥
एक नैन जस दरपन और तेहि निरमल भाउ।
सब रूपवंत पाँव गहि मुख जोवहिं कइ चाउ॥ —21

In the next stanza, he mentions his close friends, and then introduces his *Padmavat.* The introduction begins with Jayas:

'I composed this in the pious city of Jayas. I beseech scholars to ignore my mistakes. Following other poets, I have also said something. I have opened up the treasure-chest of my heart with the key of my speech. My tongue sings the praises of Ratan and the "matter" (subject matter of this work—Padmavati); and thus causes the flow of sweet nectar. One whose words carry the heart-pangs of separation, is bound to forget everything—hunger, shelter and all. He turns into a mendicant; he lives like a ruby in dust.'

जाएस नगर धरम अस्थानू। तहवाँ यह सब कीन्ह बखानू॥
औ बिनती पंडितन्ह सों भजा। टूट सँवारेहु मेरेहु सजा॥
हौं सब कबिन्ह कीर पछिलगा। किछु कहि चला तबल दइ डगा॥
हिअ भंडार नग आहि जो पूंजी। खोली जीभ तारा कै कूंजी॥
रतन पदारथ बोलइ बोला। सुरस पेम मधु भरिअ अमोला॥
जेहि के बोल बिरह के घाया। कहु तेहि भूख कहाँ तेहि छाया॥
फेरे भेस रहइ भा तपा। धूरि लपेटा मानिक छपा॥ —23

The metaphor of the ruby conveys Jayasi's familiarity with folk wisdom, in which the ruby (lal or manikya) is valued even more than a diamond in certain contexts. A worthy man is the 'lal' of the family or community; a mother calls her beloved son or daughter, 'My lal'. By comparing himself to a ruby and hinting at his own 'heart-pangs of separation', Jayasi underlines his own sense of self-worth. It is due to the mix of pain and pleasure of personal memories that Jayas—the first garden of *Aakhiri Kalaam*—has become a holy place, a pious city, in the very first line here. He concludes this stanza (23) with moving words about carrying the pain of bodily deformities along with self-confidence, quite suitable for a 'ruby in dust':

Muhammad–poet of love, ugly and frail,
causes laughters and jeers
But hearing his verses, nobody can hold back tears

(मुहम्मद कबि प्रेम का, ना तन रकत ना माँस
जिइ देखा तिइ हँसा, जौ सुना तौ आए आँस)

Significantly, this description is echoed, when love-bitten Ratansen—who is about to leave for Simhal as a yogi—describes the appearance of a true lover like himself.

Who/What is Padmini?

Padmini, in the Indian thinking on Kama—erotic desire—is the name given to the ultimate ideal of feminine beauty. Padmini is in fact an actualization of the ultimate male fantasy of feminine beauty and grace. Incidentally, not all are female, there are male prototypes also in the Kama literature.

Padmini could be a name given to a particular person, but in most of the cases, padmini is a generic term which can refer to any woman who meets the criteria. Hence, in many folk tales of north India, not only the blue-blooded royals, but even ordinary young men sometimes undertake the adventure of looking for 'a' padmini for themselves.

Just as Padmini represents the ideal of feminine beauty, grace and charm, Simhal Dweep (the island of Simhal) is the ideal of natural beauty and civic life. There is no ugliness of any kind there. All women and men are beautiful not only in bodily appearance but also in mind and soul. Jayasi yearned for beauty and serenity in real life, which was difficult to attain. We can understand Jayasi's choice of Simhal—the ultimate manifestation of serene beauty—as the place wherefrom his story was to begin.

As we have already seen, till Odisha, a traveller to Simhal is journeying within the real geography, but beyond Odisha, the movement is through mythical and imagined seas and towards a fabulous utopia. Jayasi constructs a narrative of human love and desire transforming into divine through his tale of Padmini of Simhal.

But such a narrative does not exhaust the possibility of other visions. Somebody can plan to travel to Simhal not to get a padmini, but with the hope of finding perfection in the form of Ram Himself. And to such a person, Kabir—the master of the spirituality beyond religion, the teacher of technique of finding Ram within—has some advice to offer: 'If only you strive to know and feel, He resides within, there is no need to head towards Sinhala dweep in search of Ram':

कबीर खोजी राम का गया जो स्यंघल दीप।
राम तौ घट ही भीतर रमि रह्या जौ आवे परतीत॥

Going to Simhal in search of Ram could be one odd case, but there are many folk tales in which a young man (generally a prince, but not always) is challenged (usually by a careless sister-in-law or stepmother) to go and get the padmini nari i.e. ideal woman from Simhal island if he is not satisfied with the quality or quantity of meal provided to him. The young man with hurt pride immediately leaves the meal and goes out on the adventurous journey.

Note the importance of the quality of the meal as a cause of discord. A padmini woman is supposed to be the epitome of perfection in that department as well. The male fantasy of her perfection is not confined to expertise in erotica; it values good food as well. Jayasi seems to have been a food enthusiast himself—he tends to give long-winded descriptions of feasts, exhibiting his knowledge of food culture. He particularly spends a lot of time describing the variety of cuisines at the feast organized by Ratansen for Alauddin. Such occasions provide readers wonderful insights.

Jayasi describes Simhal with great passion. At the outset, he hints at the twilight zone of reality and fantasy. Simhal, according to Jayasi, is 'indescribable, as it is like a mirror which shows you

only what you actually look like' (बरन का दरपन भाँति बिसेखा। जेहि जस रूप सो तैसेइदेखा॥).

It is also incomparable with any known island or continent including Jambudweep i.e. Indian subcontinent. As if anticipating that some readers might confuse his Simhal with Sri Lanka, he says with a touch of derision, 'Lanka is not even close to its shadow' (पूज न लंक दीप परिछाहीं।).

Jayasi does not tire of underlining the uniqueness of Simhal, he reiterates at the end of this stanza, 'None of the seven continents on the earth comes any close to Simhal' (सब संसार परचमैं आए सातौं दीप/ एकौ दीप न उत्तिम सिंघल दीप समीप).

The poet proceeds to talk about King Gandharvsen and his magnificent army, and then treats the reader with a gradually unfolding series of images of the natural as well as architectural wonders of the island, where, 'spring blossoms throughout the year'. Incidentally, Simhal's description contributes a lot to the reader's knowledge of flora and fauna.

Not only in his description of Simhal, but in the overall treatment, Jayasi sought to create such a magnificent poetic structure that 'all those men proud of their handsomeness and women proud of their beauty' feel like falling at his feet.

He needed to create a Simhal of his own words, wherein the Padmini of his poetic genius could rightfully reside.

And he did it. We know it by the name—*Padmavat*.

The light of ideal feminine beauty

Jayasi tells us, 'Padmavati was born to Champavati—wife of Gandharvsen, the king of Simhal'. He speaks of her with the reverence of a devotee. It is devotion to perfection of beauty of body, manners and soul, and he articulates it in such a moving way that many have read 'God' in Jayasi's Padmavati. As a matter of fact, he is only reminding us all of the divinity inherent in the perfect beauty of form and nobility of content i.e. soul.

Even though Padmavati is divine and she belongs to the ethereal land of Simhal, she is a mere human for whom fate has a rather strange life in store. 'She came as an inner light to Champavati's womb'; the poet tells us, but in the next line itself, we are told with an ominous touch, 'the writing of fate cannot be erased.' Then the stanza continues in a celebratory tone, going to the extent of saying that 'the island of Simhal came to light precisely because the lamp known as Padmavati illuminated it'.

The poet is playing here on the word 'deep' colloquial pronunciation of the word, dweep or island. The word deep also means lamp. The poet also says 'the jewel-illuminating abode of Shiva, came to the island of Simhal in the form of Padmavati' (दिया जो मनि सिव लोक महँ उपजा सिंघल दीप).

After the 'sixth day' (Chhathi Puja) ritual, astrologers read out Padmavati's horoscope. They describe her in superlative terms and compare her qualities and horoscope with that of Sita's.

Recall Sita's fate. She was divine grace and the purest mind personified. Her husband was an incomparable human being, God incarnate on earth. Their love went beyond any description; and yet Sita was destined to be separated from her Ram, and then leave earth before him. The unhappy turns and twists far outnumbered the happy days in Sita's life. Similar fate is indicated for Padmavati.

Ratansen's birth is not described in such superlative terms. Only at the very end, he is compared with Ram—'Ram and Sita disappeared.'

The women might be relegated to secondary position in society and its norms—but in this tale about a unique woman, Ratansen is clearly secondary to Padmavati. In the parallel universe created by Jayasi, Padmavati's status is not elevated due to her husband. It is the other way round. The poet compares Padmavati's husband with Ram because of his association with her.

Along with the Ramayana, Jayasi occasionally alludes to episodes and characters from the Mahabharata as well. In his Simhal, 'there are two rivers of neer (water) and kheer (milk) whose supply to ponds and other reservoirs in the city is as inexhaustible as the endless food in Draupadi's blessed vessel' (गढ़ पर नीर खीर दुइ नदी। पानी भरहिं जैसे दुरुपदी॥).

Astrologers also foretell Padmavati's marriage with Ratansen, at the same time declaring, 'She has descended on the island of Simhal, but will be taken by Yama (God of Death) in Jambudweep' ('सिंघल दीप भएउ अवतारू। जंबू दीप जम बारू॥').

So, at the outset itself, we are being informed that the light of ultimate beauty that descended on the utopian island of Simhal is going to be extinguished in the harsh realities of Jambudweep.

Can this not be read as a metaphor for a larger truth experienced by us all? Is it not true that the charms of our innocent dreams and fantasies meet their sudden (or slow) death in the real world of harsh realities?

At the very beginning, the poet plants twin plants of ecstasy and anxiety about the story. It is neither surprising nor unwelcome to his target audience. His readers, just like those of the Ramayana, Mahabharata or epics in Persian or other traditions, do not approach the text with suspense. They already know the outline of the story. They approach such texts again and again for the renewal of aesthetic experience and to revisit the story's connection with their own lives and emotions. Sometimes they search for consolation, sometimes confirmation for their choices and actions. In any case, they hope for a renewed energy, and often get it.

Parrot Hiraman: Friend, philosopher, guide

The narrative proceeds. Padmavati is given the best education by her doting parents. As soon as she reaches the 'marriageable' age of twelve, she is allotted a quarter of her own in the royal place and is provided with intelligent young women as companions. Her closest companion, however, is male—her favourite parrot, Hiraman. He is extremely handsome and attractive and is as intellectually inclined as Padmavati. They enjoy each other's company, and their discussion of esoteric subjects like the Vedas and Shastras is of such a high, penetrating quality that Lord Brahma (who is credited with releasing the Vedas for the benefit of human beings) himself nods in approval and appreciation:

रहहिं एक सँग दोऊ पढ़हिं सास्तर बेद
बरह्मा सीस डोलावहिं सुनत लाग सब भेद। —54

It is tempting to see Padmavati as God and Hiraman as an ideal devotee, who later on plays guru to Ratansen. But a holistic reading will not sustain this temptation; 'God' Padmavati is not able to protect Hiraman from the wrath of her father; more seriously, she is rather helpless when confronted with the evil designs of Alauddin and depends on help from the warriors Gora and Badal. Jayasi's Padmini is 'divine', but not because of any 'hidden meaning'; but due to perfection of her form and gunas—moral courage and consistency of character.

The narrative describes Hiraman and Padmini spending a lot of time together, having conversations about varied topics. Suddenly, we are told that the king is so angry with the poor parrot that he has ordered its killing. Well, it is not so sudden if one doesn't miss the subtle hint the poet gives us about what has led to the king's anger. Padmini is blossoming into a beautiful young woman, and apparently Hiraman is giving her buddhi—advice—that the king is uncomfortable with. The king is upset, as Hiraman is telling the 'moon' about the 'sun':

> राजै सुना दिस्टि भइ आना। बुधि जो देइ सँग सुआ सयाना ॥
> भएउ रजायुस मारहु सुवा। सुर सुनाव चांद जहं उआ ॥ —56

The poet is alluding to tantric terminology here. The sun stands for the male principle and the moon for the female one. Hiraman, the wise parrot, is giving Padmini knowledge about these matters and one can understand the king's anxiety, subtly hinted by Jayasi here. In the Indian erotic tradition, the parrot plays a major role and is the vehicle of the lord of love and desire, Kamadeva. Teaching a parrot to mimic human tongue is one of the sixty-four arts recommended for the nayak and nayika (the ideal lover and beloved) in the *Kama Sutra*. Then we have Shuka-Sarika Samvad (chit-chat between parrot and mynah) which resonates even today in cultural memory by its vernacular name—'Tota Mynah Ki Kahani'. In this 'discussion' between the parrot and mynah, they are both accusing each other's gender of carrying the trait of infidelity.

The parrot's role in erotic art in no way contradicts its capacity to participate in, and impart knowledge, of other disciplines. Only a couple of centuries before Jayasi, the parrots were portrayed as experts in practical matters and philosophical wisdom in *Katha*

Saritsagar. Later, we hear the great poet Keshavdas (seventeenth century CE) lamenting his choice of vernacular as the language for his compositions, while in his lineage, even the parrots and mynahs of household discoursed in Sanskrit! As a matter of fact, parrots have been reputed to possess wisdom since the Vedic era and were known as the 'wise and holy birds from India' in ancient Greece and Persia.

This image of parrots integrating erotic expertise with knowledge of other matters and general wisdom feeds into Jayasi's imagination of Hiraman. Coming back to the story, Padmini pleads for Hiraman's life and is able to send back the servants ordered by her father to eliminate the parrot.

But for how long is she able to save him from the wrath of the king? Padmini reassures Hiraman, underlining the 'dharam preeti' i.e. genuine affection between two friends, despite the fact that one is human while the other is a bird. Having 'reassured' her dear friend, she in her innocence leaves for 'Mansarovar' to enjoy some water sports with her companions.

The poet takes this opportunity to undertake a most evocative description of divinity inherent in the perfection of feminine form. Having described the carefree sport of vivacious young girls in which Padmini's necklace goes missing, much to her distress, the poet continues:

Mansarovar says, 'I got what I desired, the paras (philosopher's stone) of beauty came upto me, the touch of her feet took away all impurities of my mind,

Looking at her I too became beautiful; sandal-like fragrance of her body took away wounds and burnings of my heart. I wonder,

Who is this person bringing such fragrant, purifying air to me and making my sins go away?' At this very moment Padmavati's necklace floated over the water, her companions immediately picked it up and seeing this, she chuckled. This made the companions blossom just as water lilies do as soon as the moon rises. In fact, whosoever saw Padmavati became part of her beauty. Everyone got his or her desired form, all the faces became mirrors for the moon that Padmavati was.

One who saw her eyes turned into lotus, one who saw her form turned into crystalline water. One who saw her laughing turned into swan, the shine of her teeth was as luminous as the shine of diamonds.

(कहा मानसर चहा सो पाई। पारस रूप इहाँ लगि आई॥
भा निरमर तेन्ह पायन परसें। पाया रूप रूप के दरसें॥
मलै समीर बास तन आई। भा सीतल गै तपन बुझाई॥
न जनौ कौनु पौन लै आवा। पुन्नि दसा भै पाप गँवावा॥
ततखन हार बेगि उतराना। पावा सखिन्ह चंद बिहँसाना॥
बिगसे कुमुद देखि ससि रेखा। भै तेंहि रूप जहाँ जो देखा॥
पाए रूप रूप जस चहे। ससि मुख सब दरपन होइ रहे॥
नैन जो देखे कँवल भए निरमर नीर सरीर।
हँसत जो देखे हंस भए दसन जोति नग हीर॥) —65

Note, *Padmavati's beauty makes its beholder also beautiful instead of demeaning her/him. It is 'divine' because it adds to human potential instead of diminishing it.*

She is 'beautiful' not only due to her perfect female form, but also because of paras-like (paras by its touch, is supposed to turn base metal into gold) qualities of her soul. She personifies that part of Jayasi's praises to the Lord wherein he expresses gratitude to Him for creating some human beings as carriers and active spreaders of positivity.

Back in the palace, despite Padmavati's assurance, Hiraman is wise enough to know that, 'no bird can survive in a place where a cat has been let loose'; he flies away, leaving a lamenting Padmini behind, who is told by her servants that the parrot was killed by a cat.

Hiraman flies away from the paradox of Padmavati's doting love and her father's life-threatening displeasure; and comes to his own—the birds in the jungle. He finds real empathy there and genuinely regrets leaving his own people 'in search of selfish pleasure'. All the birds lament their fate in a world of 'men'; attributing their plight of being easy prey to men to their own indiscretion. Like any lamentation of the powerless in the world of the powerful, it ends in a hapless quietude: 'No point in saying anything now, better just keep quiet' (अब कहना किछु नाहीं मस्ट भली पक्षिराज).

Chapter 2

Ratansen and Chittor

Hiraman, the wise bird

After the lamentations of helpless birds, the poet brings us back to the world of humans—this time in Chittor. Quite significantly, there is only one stanza describing the birth of the epic's hero. Chitrasen, the king of Chittor, is blessed with a son named Ratansen, and the astrologers foretell his singular achievement—'He will go as a yogi to Simhal and will bring Padmini to Chittor.'

The poet could not have been clearer in underlining the centrality of Padmini to the narrative. After this brief description of the hero's arrival in the scene, the story goes back to Hiraman, who connects the utopian island of Simhal with Chittor of the real world. Apparently, *Padmavat*'s structure can be divided into two parts—the first belonging to the realm of fable and the second to the sphere of history. Simhal, Padmini and her parrot are part of the fable, while the capture of Chittor by Alauddin is a recorded historical event. It is important to remember, however, that Jayasi himself has not used any such division of 'imaginary' and 'historical' of the stanzas. It is later scholars who have divided it into thematic khands of varying sizes for convenience.

There is no point in reading *Padmavat* as a historical text. It must be read as what it really is—a great work of the imagination using the historical so that the audience can relate to it more intimately. For Jayasi, the historical is Gadharudha Pratyaya (a narrative well-entrenched in popular memory)—nothing more, nothing less. That is why Jayasi did not face any problem in connecting imaginary Simhal with real Chittor. Both are integral to his narrative.

The entire narration in its integrity is equally real or imaginary for his creative intent. He did not intend to write down a Sufi allegory, nor was he writing a bardic poem valorizing any of the conflicting parties. His poetic sympathies are with Padmini and Ratansen, not because he desired to valorize any notion of Rajput or Hindu honour, but because their love is true and for that they suffer tragically and through no fault of their own.

The poetical integrity of *Padmavat* has suffered a lot due to the modern inability of handling its structural integrity in a sensitive manner. Those who read it in order to find historical evidence for their own political stances neglect the miraculous, so-called imaginary (as opposed to historical) part of the story. That is why the island of Simhal is either located in Rajasthan or equated with Sri Lanka. Such people are hard-pressed to explain the role of Hiraman—which is so crucial in the narrative. Or perhaps, prefer to forget him altogether as is the case with a recent, opulent film, claiming to be based on Jayasi's *Padmavat*.

On the other hand, those who read it as a Sufi poem end up reducing all the characters to lifeless symbols, depriving them of their fulsome humanness. They deny the text its humanizing poignancy.

To bring Hiraman to Chittor, the poet introduces a Brahmin. In order to make some money, he joins a group of banjaras or gypsy traders going to Simhal. Simhal—the land of abundant prosperity—is a great commercial centre. Jayasi describes the vibrant markets of Simhal with gusto. The poor Brahmin soon realizes he is too small a fry to do any commerce in such a market. The group of banjaras is getting ready to leave for home. The

Brahmin is wandering around when at that very moment, a fowler comes to market. Amongst his goods there is an exceptionally attractive parrot; the Brahmin ends up talking to him. 'Why should you hide your qualities, I am a pundit and you seem to be one yourself. Why don't you tell me something about yourself? After all, a scholar can open up to another scholar.'

The parrot opens up; it is the same Hiraman who only a little while ago was seen with other free birds lamenting their haplessness in the world of men, unsure of when their freedom would come to an end.

'With my freedom lost, all my qualities are also gone,' Hiraman tells the Brahmin. 'What qualities can I boast of in this state of captivity? I have been put in a cage and I am on sale. A true scholar does not bring himself to the market for sale, one who does so loses his knowledge. I can see two ways from this market; I do not know which one has been chosen for me by destiny... I have earned immense knowledge, but what use is all that when

I am uncertain of my life? At this moment, the haze around me has numbed my intellect.'

The Brahmin is moved by the parrot's grief; he buys him and starts his journey back home. By the time he reaches Chittor, Chitrasen has passed away and Ratansen is the new king. He comes to know about Hiraman—the parrot—who is reputed to be as knowledgeable as Sahadeva (one of the five Pandava brothers known for his scholarly achievements) and as gifted as Vyasa (the author of the Mahabharata and all the Puranas). 'Such a unique bird belongs to the palace, not to the humble abode of a poor Brahmin,' the king orders the Brahmin, who reluctantly parts company with Hiraman. The Brahmin is richly compensated for it.

This is how Hiraman travels from Padmavati's abode in the utopia of Simhal to the earthly palace of Ratansen, via the route destined for birds—being captured, sold and bought—which even wise ones like Hiraman cannot escape.

Nagmati's anguish

As expected, the king is deeply impressed with Hiraman, who 'either speaks words as luminous and valuable as the rubies and corals, or just keeps his tongue tied' (जौ बोलै तो मानिक मूँगा। नाहिं तो मौन बाँध होइ गूँगा॥).

Little wonder that the parrot who acts as a hero's guide and a poet's voice is given to either speaking meaningfully or not speaking at all. After all, his creator Jayasi knew the value of words and the virtue of silence only too well.

But there are moments when even Hiraman cannot stay quiet. Soon enough, he finds himself in such a moment, where he becomes the tool to take the narrative further. One day, when Ratansen is away, his queen Nagmati adorns herself and standing in front of the mirror, she asks a variant of the question—'Mirror, mirror on the wall/Who is the fairest of them all?' The difference, however, is that here the question is not addressed to the mirror, (which has in any case satisfied her by giving the desired answer), but to the pundit parrot from the island of Simhal. She questions him and challenges him to reply on oath, 'You are supposed to be an expert assayer; now, use your touchstone, take oath by the king, and tell me: is there anyone more beautiful in your Simhal? Is that Padmavati (of whom you think so much) anywhere close to me?'

Hiraman initially intends to avoid the tricky situation by giving some diplomatic answer. But Nagmati's insistence on the comparison to the women of Simhal, in particular Padmavati, takes away all his diplomacy; and then there is also the oath involving the well-being of his benefactor, Ratansen. He bursts out rather derisively—'Where is the question of comparison with the women of Simhal? Of course, in a pond, which is never visited by swans, herons can claim to be swans. But really, can one compare day with night? The Simhal women have fragrant bodies, and as far as Padmavati is concerned, her body has the complexion of purified gold and is blessed with a unique fragrance.'

Hiraman then tries to balance his blunt words with consoling ones, 'What is the point of such a comparison? Any woman desired by her man is beautiful. Isn't she?' But the damage has been done. Nagmati cannot bear the truth and is mad with jealousy and insecurity and decides to have Hiraman eliminated. Nagmati knows the nature of men, particularly, kings. She is also aware of the 'incidents' of men leaving for Simhal in search of padmini women. She comes to a conclusion—sooner than later, Hiraman is 'going to tell Ratansen about Padmini, and then, the king is certainly going to become a yogi and leave Chittor in search of Padmini'.

She instructs her reliable maidservant to take the wretched bird away and kill it in such a way that not a single soul witnesses the act. The maid takes the parrot, but unlike her mistress, she reflects over the situation calmly: 'In the first place, one cannot kill someone admired by the king . Secondly, what wrong has this poor parrot committed? He is a pundit; in fact, he seems to be a renunciate who is here due to some break in his sadhana. How

can I kill this parrot on the order of a woman who is not even bothered about her husband's affection for it? If and when he orders a search for this parrot, I will have to face the music.'

As soon as the king returns, he ask Nagmati about Hiraman, who answers arrogantly. 'I was just curious about Padmini of Simhal,' she says, 'and the impertinent parrot told me that compared to her, I was like a snake, like night compared to day. In fact, he said that my husband was also like an owl who could not appreciate the bright beauty of the day. My Lord, what a sharp tongue this tiny bird has; how crooked he is! Perhaps that's why his face is red—from sucking people's blood. It is good-looking, but can we pamper such an evil bird? What use is gold that hurts the ears?'

Through Ratansen's fond remembrance of Hiraman, Jayasi describes the qualities of scholars and the value of their friendship. Ratansen is grief-stricken because of the loss of a scholar friend. Being an angry husband as well as a king, he says—'Having done this, don't think you are going to be happy. Either make the dead bird alive, or go and commit sati with him.'

Nagmati is stunned and realizes that she has been defeated even before the 'battle' has formally begun. Her maid who had defied her order to kill Hiraman comes to help. Nagmati ends up getting scolded from her friendly maid as well. The parrot is handed over to the king. Nagmati is hurt and her disillusionment with her husband comes out in moving words of exasperation, 'I thought I meant a lot to you, but obviously, to you, this bird is more important than me. You ordered your wife to commit sati with him if he could not be brought back to life. My dear husband, I loved and served you all my life and was proud of our love, but this is the reward I get. Well, at least now I know the truth—you are with me, but do not belong to me. You are here only in appearance but actually, seem from an alien land. So strange you seem to me now. But, anyway, I will do what you want...'

At this point, the illusion of exclusive love and devotion lost, Nagmati is experiencing a heartbreaking 'strangeness'. Significantly, Jayasi has reconstructed Nagmati's pain in words, similes and metaphors carrying spiritual overtone. Perhaps it is a poetic device to lessen the load of his own bitter memories of the strangeness he experienced in the behaviour of someone in the 'first garden'.

In fact, it is this point onwards that the events, descriptions and dialogues are constructed as if the poet is trying to point out something important to his readers. He is constantly trying to remind his audience that more often than not, the so-called 'spiritual experience' is a metamorphosis of precisely what Nagmati at this moment is experiencing in her human love.

Though dejected, Nagmati is never completely vanquished. Even after Padmavati's arrival at the royal abode, she continues to fight for her space. People who read *Padmavat* as an allegory of Sufi spiritualism see her character as symbolic of worldly bonds. This is being insensitive to a woman who was forced to suffer for absolutely no fault of hers. Whatever the interpreters may say, in the poet's narrative, she comes out as a human being who deserves sympathy. To Jayasi, she is not someone to be derided or considered as an evil person symbolizing any undesirable bond. Jayasi's description of her longing for Ratansen, while he is enjoying his new-found love in Simhal, is considered one of the finest pieces of poetry of longing and pain in Hindi literature.

To describe Nagmati's pain of separation, Jayasi has used the device of looking at the change of seasons from the longing beloved's (or lover's) point of view. Used by Kalidasa and later poets, this trope, by Jayasi's time, had become an important literary device and part of popular culture. This device is called Barahmasa (i.e. description of twelve months) and is used in *Padmavat* with Jayasi's unique signature.

The parrot describes Padmavati to Ratansen

Ratansen knows that the truth sometimes hurts, but being a king, he knows only too well that powerful people are in the habit of shutting those who speak the truth. He wants to know the truth behind what has made Nagmati so angry. 'Without truth, human being is hollow,' he tells Hiraman, 'without truth, dharma does not hold. Only that who is bent upon destroying dharma can abandon truth. In fact, the whole world holds together due to truth.'

Hiraman's response is typical in its forthrightness and once again, he puts his adoration of Padmini in bold relief. 'Padmavati is the daughter of king of Simhal. She glows like purified gold and her body is fragrant like lotus; all the padminis of Simhal are just her shadows. I, Hiraman, happen to be her dear bird; by serving her, I got my speech, otherwise I would have remained dumb forever.'

Padmavati's beauty is the Truth of Hiraman—the wise bird.

Hiraman thanks this truth of beauty for all his qualities. His gratitude to Padmavati is articulated in the most moving words—'I will remember her day and night as long as I live; even while dying, I will take her memories with me. I will carry to the other world my body which she has made green and my mouth which she has made red':

(जौ लहि जिऔं रात-दिन सुमिरौं मरौं तो ओहि लै जाऊं।
मुख राता तन हरिअर कीन्हे ओहूँ जगत लै जाऊँ ॥) —93

The wordplay here is a challenge to the translator. Acquiring a green hue (the verb हरियाना) is an idiomatic metaphor for getting reinvigorated; and a red hue signifies fulfilment.

Indian folk wisdom sees parrots as very self-centred creatures. The absence of gratitude is considered a parrot's second nature. Given this popular image, Hiraman's gratitude is even more compelling and moving. The bond of love and friendship between Padmavati and Hiraman permeates this epic in such an evocative manner that every sensitive reader ends up longing for at least one such bond of friendship in his/her own life.

Padmavat *is not just about Ratansen and Padmini. It is also about Hiraman and Padmavati. It is not just about a man-woman love, it is also about true friendship.*

To read or reconstruct *Padmavat* without Hiraman—the parrot—is not only missing the link between Padmavati and Ratansen, but also ignoring a beautiful relationship of faith and sharing.

Falling in love by listening about or looking at a picture of the hero or heroine was a traditional poetic convention. By now, Ratansen is 'in love' with Padmavati. But he is immediately cautioned by Hiraman, 'Don't get any wrong ideas, king, the path of love is very difficult to follow. Only those willing to give away their head can rightfully talk of love' (पेम सुनत मन भूलु न राजा। कठिन पेम सिर देइ तौ छाजा॥). This immediately brings Kabir to mind—'This is the abode of love, not your aunt's home. Only he who cuts off his head himself and places it on the ground can hope to enter' (कबिरा यहु घर प्रेम का खाला का घर नाहिं। सीस उतारै, भुइं धरै, तब पैजै घर मांहि।).

At this point, the poet underlines the difference between real love and mere infatuation. Ratansen has fallen in love in a conventional way all right, but he insists on being different; refuses to be dispirited. We continue to hear the echoes of Kabir in Ratansen when he says, 'I know how arduous the path of love is, but one who traverses it gives meaning to his life and afterlife. Within suffering is stored the nectar of love. It is meant only for those who are ready to face even death. What is the point of coming to earth if you never take the road to love? I have taken this road, and will remain steadfast on it. Please be my guide, don't abandon me. Only he who has seen the door to love can guide others to it. You cannot know love without experiencing it. Yes, one has to suffer acutely on this way; but only till you meet your beloved. Once you meet her/him, the sorrows accumulated over many births go away.

You have seen her; please describe her beauty head to toe. God willing, I will be able to meet her.'

(भलेहिं पेम है कठिन दुहेला। दुइ जग तरा पेम जेइँ खेला॥
दुख भीतर जो पेम मधु राखा। गंजन मरन सहै सो चाखा॥
जेइ नहिँ सीस पेम पंथ लावा। सो प्रिथिमी महँ काहे कों आवा॥
अब मैं प्रेम पंथ सिर मेला। पाँव न टेलु राखु कै चेला॥

प्रेम बार कहै जो देखा। जेइँ न देखा का जाना बिसेखा॥
तब लगि दुख प्रीतम नहिँ भेंटा। जब भेंटा जरमन्ह दुख मेटा॥
असि अनूप तुइँ देखी नख सिख बरनि सिंगार।
है मोंहि आस मिलन कै जो मेरवैं करतार॥) —98

What is the point of coming to this earth, if you never take the road to love?

This is Jayasi's core concern and the central theme of his epic. Ratansen, the king, will don the appearance of a yogi, following the guidance of a parrot; he will brave the most ferocious ocean, the Kilkila, on the way to Simhal. Having reached there, he will confront each and every obstacle, even face the potential self-immolation and probable execution.

Jayasi composed his epic to celebrate love which, if practised properly, even makes the member of a supposedly ungrateful species—Hiraman the parrot—feel grateful to his friend and mistress in this life and beyond. Love, due to which, a wife (Nagmati) who has been deeply hurt, still longs in pain for her husband.

Requested by Ratansen, Hiraman proceeds to describe Padmavati; and the reader is treated with Jayasi's brilliant exposition of yet another poetic convention—'Nakh-shikh Varnan' i.e. head-to-toe description of a beautiful lady. This runs into several stanzas and every limb of her body is described through conventional similes and metaphors, but with a 'Jayasi' touch. The parting between the heroine's hair is traditionally seen as a golden mark on the touchstone or likened to lightning by poets; but for Jayasi, it is like River Saraswati underlying River Yamuna. (Saraswati is the invisible 'third' river, Ganga and Yamuna are two visible ones at the confluence of three rivers—

Triveni—at Prayag i.e. Allahabad in U.P.; and Yamuna is supposed to be dark in colour.) Though the smooth and soft back of the nayika has been praised by many, Jayasi constructs a word-image of Padmavati looking slightly backwards while moving. This image immediately brings to mind a pose of female form very popular with the sculptors in medieval and early modern India. (Recall the female forms in Khajuraho and Konark). Hiraman concludes the description of Padmini's body with these words, 'I just could not do justice to that pure beauty, there is nothing in the world which can work as a proper simile.'

The ultimate Jayasi touch in the tip-to-toe description, however, lies in the fact that his Padmavati is not merely a unique beauty, but has great intellect as well.

Hiraman tells Ratansen that besides full knowledge of Vedas, Padmini also has command over *Amarkosha* (Sanskrit thesaurus composed by Amarsimha in fourth century CE), Mahabharata, Gita and the art of Rhetoric. Even pundits cannot match her in interpreting these texts. She also knows Bhaswati (a school of astrology), grammar and Puranas. She reaches the essence of these discourses as directly as a piercing arrow. She is virtually like Saraswati (the goddess of knowledge) in her learning.'

(अमर भारथ पिंगल औ गीता। अरथ जूझ पंडित नहिं जीता॥
भावसती व्याकरण सरसुती पिंगल पाठ पुरान।
बेद भेद सैं बात कह तस जनु लागहिं बान॥) —108

'I must leave...'

Ratansen is beside himself. He must bring Padmini to his life; he must travel to Simhal *now*. Family members, courtiers, ministers, elders of the community—none can make Ratansen 'see sense'; he is not listening to anyone. No medicines are working. If at all he talks, he talks only of his love which has made him indifferent to every relation, every pleasure—a renunciate. The poet here chooses words which carry significance beyond Ratansen's condition. We see Ratansen crying like a baby and hear him saying something which echoes our inner voice, 'I originally belonged to city of life, how come I left it? How come I lost true knowledge (of my real self)? I was in the city of eternal life, how come I find myself here in the city of dead?'

(आवन जगत बालक जस रोवा। उठा रोइ हो ग्यान सो खोवा॥
हौं तो अहा अमरपुर जहाँ। इहाँ अरनपुर आएहुँ कहाँ॥) —121

Ratansen has to leave for the city of eternal life, the island of Padmavati—Simhal. However, Hiraman is quite straightforward, in fact, rude in his warning,

'Going to Simhal is not that easy, king, it is not like taking a meal at home. Only he who is willing to give up his life should dare take the route to Simhal. Only a yogi, a Sanyasi, a seeker can take that route. Love is like a difficult mountain, where the sulis (a kind of gibbet—the piercing iron rods on which the humans were impaled) come up as sprouts. Either the thieves or (the noble souls like) Mansur are impaled on them. You are a king, given to pleasures and privileges. If at all you want to do some sadhana, why bother about Padmavati of Simhal? Your own body has ten doors through which things of essence are being robbed day in and day out. Come to your senses and save your possessions from the robbers.'

'Mansur' mentioned by Hiraman was a Sufi impaled on a gibbet in Baghdad in the tenth century. What Hiraman is telling here is very significant. He is talking about those with power and authority who treat the act of love as a crime. They send Mansur (representative here of all genuine lovers) to gallows along with robbers.

(Is this not true even today—in the era of khap and caste panchayats issuing dictates of so-called 'honour killings' and young lovebirds being hounded every day?)

Jayasi is also making an important point against the world views that dismiss human emotions as distractions from the 'true' path. The contrasting world view is defined by the fact that love, as a sentiment perforce, reaches out to the 'other' who becomes even more important than the 'self'. You prioritize his or her happiness and well-being over your own. Such a world view enriches one's inner search by adding a social dimension to it. Kabir and many others who shared this world view worked on the inner principle persistently and at the same time related it with society quite insistently. They voiced their criticism of social and religious ills—loud and clear.

Jayasi also shares this world view, though in a different manner. Instead of vociferously criticizing, he makes a nuanced poetic statement in favour of human love and reiterates the point made by Kabir, 'Far from being a sin, the erotic desire can actually orient one to the divine'. After entering into this vaikunth of spiritual upliftment, all kinds of prejudices—religious and otherwise—fall aside. However, only those with great perseverance can hope to achieve the kind of manush prem (human love) that will turn both the lover and the beloved into vaikunthi (divine) beings.

In the present dialogue, the poet has assigned Hiraman the role of stating the 'given position' (Purva Paksha) of those who insist solely on the inner principle and ignore love as a distraction. Ratansen is assigned the task of reiterating the poet's own position (Siddhanta Paksha). Ratansen does reiterate the poet's position and most appropriately, not in words but in his resolve for action. He briefly responds to Hiraman's long discourse saying, 'Yes, I know all the hazards, but I will still undertake the journey to Simhal to have Padmavati, even if it means giving away not only pleasures of royal life, but life itself.'

Ratansen becomes a yogi, a sadhaka—not of hath-yoga, but of love-yoga. Instead of taking him to the solitude of some dark cave, his love-yoga takes him to the city illuminated with the light of the most beautiful woman—Padmavati.

The love-yogi's voyage

Jayasi provides details of the clothes and manner, possessions and practices of yogis when describing Ratansen's as a yogi—from the special ash covering their bodies and their huge earrings to their uttering the name of Gorakhnath. Famous yogis—Gopichand and Bhartihari—are also mentioned as examples of renunciation and focus of mind. Jayasi also takes this opportunity to typically convey (or display, if you please) his knowledge of omens. There are good omens all around: a person is bringing curd and fish in a silver pot, a young woman is carrying a pot filled with water over her head, a deer is approaching from the right side, a gardener-woman is bringing her peacock; and the wagtail bird (khanjan) is seen sitting on a snake's head.

Ratansen tells his mother as well as Nagmati that his resolution is irrevocable. To his mother, with some politeness, to Nagmati, with expected derision, as he is still upset with her, and being his wife, she is a 'natural' obstacle in the way of his desire to reach the other woman—Padmavati. Jayasi constructs this scene with sympathy to Nagmati who promises to serve and please her husband until her end. She implores Ratansen to stay back, pensively asking, 'Is "she" really more attractive than me?' Her desperate appeal to the yogi-king's 'reason' is heart-wrenching.

'I know men by nature have eyes on many women, but how can you ditch the ones you already know. We all bless you, please stay back, rule over Chittor and preserve our fortunes':

> (भवै भलेहिं पुरुष की दीठी। जिन्ह जाना तिन्हु न पीठी।
> देहि असीस सबै मिलि तुम्ह माथैं निति छात।
> राज करहु गढ़ चितउर राखहु पिय अहिवात ॥) —131

Jayasi has constructed Padmavati's character as an epitome of feminine charm and beauty; but it is Nagmati who epitomizes the real plight of women in a patriarchal system.

The poetic brilliance of Jayasi lies in his act of giving Nagmati an important voice instead of sidelining or silencing her in his Padmavati-centric narration.

Ratansen's advisers and court-priests try to dissuade him or at least postpone his departure for a more opportune moment. Ratansen responds with firmness typical of someone obsessed with something. He says, 'A lover does not look at the auspicious moments, he moves as soon as he comes to know (of love). Pundits get into so much thinking of this and that moment being appropriate. They just forget that death does not bother itself with such questions about the moment. She takes away anyone, including pundits.'

The determined love-yogi departs, leaving behind a 'dance of grief'.

It is in this context that Ratansen describes the appearance of a true lover in the words evoking the memory of the poet's self-description—'A lover's body has almost no flesh, no blood either, his body is pale and tears in his eyes are dried up' (जेहि तन पेम कहाँ तेहि माँसू। कया न रकत न नयननिन्ह आँसू॥).

Although Ratansen is now a love-yogi, he is still a king and so, he leaves his palace in style. He sounds the singi (a typical instrument of yogis) like a general heading an army of 'thousands' (obviously a rhetorical exaggeration) of yogis. These are the feudal lords who are following Ratansen out of affection or perhaps, and this is more likely, due to the age-old convention of princes accompanying their king. This army of yogis, headed by the one intoxicated by love, marches on in their journey uninterrupted and at a fast pace, following Hiraman's able guidance. It is in his words of guidance that Hiraman indicates the route to Simhal which lies in the ocean beyond Odisha. (Upon his arrival, as mentioned earlier, the king, of the Gajapati dynasty, will welcome Ratansen and supply him with a fleet of his best ships.)

The idea of 'seven seas' has been a part of the idiom of language. Kabir wanted to turn the water of all the seven seas into ink in order to write the praises of Ram, but given his divine grandeur, found the exercise inadequate. From folk songs to film songs, the trope of seven seas appears to convey large distance and sometimes an abundance. Jayasi invests this idea with additional meaning, but before that, he also hints that he is conversant with sailors' tales as well. Our poet seems to have been a walking encyclopaedia, having insights about almost everything under the sun. Even Tulsidas, otherwise quite knowledgeable, does not appear to have been as familiar with Islamic beliefs, traditions, mythologies and legends.

Rejection in love in 'first garden' indeed does wonders to a poetic soul!

Jayasi reminds us of the inner connection of the seven seas which are at the same time different and autonomous. The first

five consist of water, milk, curd, fire, and wine respectively. Then comes the most ferocious one—the Kilkila, and finally Mansar. These seven seas symbolize the levels of various attachments and challenges, and the Kilkila, indicating the final confusion just before achieving clarity, is the most ferocious. The powerful ones and the achievers are more likely to deviate from the right path than those who have not been able to overcome the earlier difficulties. The reason is simple; the achiever has the added load of pride after crossing the first five seas successfully. Hiraman tells Ratansen, 'The right moral compass and the real guru is urgently required at this point; it is here that people lose their essence. The reason that almost nobody reaches Simhal is precisely because they cannot negotiate the Kilkila which is as confusing as it is ferocious. It gives you life and death, hope and despair. One who drowns can't help going to the darkest depths; one who is able to negotiate it is bound to reach the paradise.'

Ratansen need not worry. His moral compass is set right and he is blessed with the right guru in Hiraman. His 'army' reaches the seventh sea—the Mansar—unscathed. A view of the Mansar takes away the pains and tiredness of the voyagers. Their steadfast commitment to the truth has paid off finally. They feel as if they are seeing the dawn for the first time, and now Simhal is very much in sight.

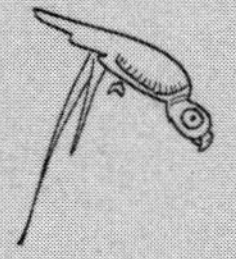

Chapter 3

The Hero in Utopia

Ratansen's tapasya

Ratansen and his army of yogis are absolutely stunned by the beauty and splendour of Simhal. They can't believe their senses as they perceive the incredible. There is a mountain of gold, the sun and the moon seem to appear simultaneously in sky, the wind is fragrant with sandal and so on...

'Where have we reached?' Ratansen wonders.

Hiraman while addressing Ratansen's query takes the opportunity to introduce him to the company of great sadhakas (yogis and kings) who through their perseverance in the commitment to truth have made great marks on collective memory. He mentions King Vikramaditya (celebrated for his dispensation of justice), Harishchandra (revered for his devotion to truth and his word), and of course, the great yogis Macchindarnath i.e Matsyendranath and his disciple Gorakhnath, apart from Gopichand and Bhartihari. Hiraman congratulates him, 'You have conquered both earth and sky, and now you have Simhal in sight.'

Ratansen can get the chance of having the 'first darshan' of Padmini only when she ventures out of the fort. Fortunately, the fifth day of the month Magha—Vasant Panchmi—is not far, and that is the day she comes to worship at the Shiva temple. Vasant Panchmi is the day of celebrating the god of erotic desire—Madan or Kamadeva—and the goddess of knowledge—Saraswati. For Ratansen, the first look of Padmavati will signify the fructification of his voyage which—as we have seen—has been constructed by Jayasi as an intertwined search for the epitome of feminine beauty and the sense of self. It is worth remembering Hiraman's description of Padmavati—she is supremely beautiful, said to be like Saraswati in her academic excellence. Thus, Ratansen receiving his first 'darshan' of her on Vasant Panchmi is all the more significant.

He has to climb a hill to reach the Shiva Temple. 'What is a hill? I can run and climb upto the sky in order to see her,' Ratansen tells Hiraman. He also says something universally applicable to efforts, successes and failures—'One who aims high, goes up day by day; one should never give up the determination of aiming high, even if one has to sometimes suffer falls':

(दिन दिन ऊँच होइ सो जेहि ऊंचे पर चाउ।
ऊँचे चढ़त परिअ जौं ऊँच न छाड़िय काउ॥) —163

Hiraman now flies towards Padmavati's palace. Ratansen—the love-yogi—cannot wait; he along with his fellow yogis immediately climb the hill and reach the Shiva Temple.

The core statement of Jayasi's *Padmavat* is made here at the temple of Shiva—whose name literally means 'beneficent'.

Shiva had also gone 'mad' in love for his wife—Sati. Her father Daksha Prajapati had rather tense relations with her husband. Once he organized a yajna, but did not invite Shiva and Sati. She thought it was an inadvertent mistake and reached her father's place. Then she realized that not inviting her and her husband was actually deliberate. Feeling humiliated, she committed suicide. This led to tremendous grief and devastating anger on Shiva's part, who could be pacified only after great efforts by all the devas.

In response to ceaseless supplications from Ratansen, we hear a divine voice, in fact the word used by the poet is akoot (अकूत), literally meaning 'incalculable'. This voice of incalculable value addresses Ratansen, but not only him: 'It is love that turns a human being, who is otherwise nothing but a handful of dust, into the divine. Love gives both the nectar of life (rasa) as well as the pain of suffering; just as in a beehive you get honey as well as the stings. You may not get true love even if you go looking for it, and you could find it sitting at home; the point is true dedication.'

(कै अस्तुति जौं बहुत मनावा। सबद अकूत मंडप महँ आवा ॥
मानुस पेम भएउ बैकुंठी। नाहिं त काह छार एक मूँठी ॥
पेमहि माहँ बिरह औ रसा। मैन के घर मधु अंब्रित बसा ॥
निसत धाइ जौं मरै तो काहा। सत जौं करै बैसेइ लाहा ॥) —166

Encouraged by the divine approval of his love, Ratansen spreads out his yogi's tiger-skin, sits on it and starts chanting the name of his love—Padmavati. With his mind solely focused on her, he soon goes into a state of trance—samadhi. He performs such a tapasya that his clothes burn due to the fire of love inside his being. He somehow wishes to reach his love, even if it is 'by turning into dust and reaching her door with the wind!'

The mesmerizing Padmavati

Love works in mysterious ways. The vibes generated by Ratansen's great desire and his fierce tapasya reach Padmavati, even before anyone tells her about Ratansen. It is as if the whole universe is whispering into her ears that the man suitable for her is close by. She experiences pangs of longing for the man (still unnamed as far as she is concerned) who is waiting for her darshan in the Shiva temple. She opens her heart to no one, except her maid, who is sympathetic but at the same time cautions Padmavati of love's difficult terrain.

Padmavati has an intuition that this Vasant Panchmi is going to be very special. She is looking forward to it and is experiencing pangs of longing for the one—who she still does not know.

At this point, Hiraman makes his entry. Padmavati is beside herself with joy. Having exchanged notes of the time since when Hiraman escaped the wrath of her father and reached Ratansen's place, they come to the point of Padmavati's mysterious 'affliction'. Hiraman informs her about Ratansen, 'Blessed are his parents to have such a son. He is the king of Chittor, possesses all the thirty-two signs of a great king and is as suitable for you as gold is for a jewel. I have told him about you, and now, there is an inextinguishable flame of desire for you in his heart. For your love, he has turned into a yogi, relinquishing his kingdom. He is as resplendent as the sun and you are like the philosopher's stone. Your union is destined by God Himself; I have only acted as an instrument of the divine plan.'

Jayasi compares Padmavati with paras-patthar, the philosopher's stone, several times in the text. This is his way of underlining the transformative qualities of her beauty and personality.

Finally, after a long wait on the part of the lover and beloved, the day of Vasant Panchmi arrives. Padmavati leaves to worship Shiva, accompanied by many women. Here too, Jayasi's description provides important historical information. He describes the dresses and gaits of the 'women from thirty-six castes' accompanying Padmavati. The first one mentioned is a 'Kori' woman in a patola silk garment. Koris were Hindu weavers and were known for their dexterity with silk. Theoretically, in the caste schema, Koris are not very high, but a Kori woman being put first in the list of royal companions indicates the difference between theoretical dictates and real practice. The textile trade and industry played a crucial role in the economy of early modern India of Jayasi's times. It is not surprising that a woman of a

community involved in this trade gets priority over a Brahmin woman in Jayasi's enumeration. These two are followed by women belonging to the Agrawal, Baisa, Chandel, Chauhan, goldsmith, wine-seller, grocer, and beetle-leaf seller castes. The professions of all the castes mentioned here have some connection with the pleasures and riches of life.

Enjoying themselves on the way, this group of vivacious young women reaches Shiva's Temple. In the temple, the Gods look at her and all their sins go away. Padmavati, when offering her puja, is naturally praying for her wish fulfilment, and the poet comments, 'Who will respond to her request? God is dead, only an indefinable voice making this announcement is echoing in the temple.' (उत्तर को देइ देव मरि गएऊ। सबद अकूत मँडप महँ भएऊ।) Needless to say, 'dead' is a metaphor for the deity being left stunned and speechless in the presence of the epitome of feminine beauty—Padmavati.

Padmavati chuckles with understandable delight, 'Well, I wanted to offer my puja to this God, now who is going to accept it?' At this moment, a companion comes and informs Padmavati about a strange sight—a yogi is sitting at the eastern gate of the temple, he seems to be a prince with all the thirty-two qualities.

Padmavati rushes to the eastern gate, and when she casts a glance at Ratansen, she knows intuitively who he is. Ratansen, as radiant as the sun, is in meditation at the moment, unaware of the fact that the one whom he is mediating for is in his midst. In this brief episode, we see Padmavati once again conscious of the impact of her beauty and charm, 'I don't venture out of my house as anyone I cast a glance on departs from the world out of sheer pleasure and excitement.' She also chuckles at Ratansen's ironical situation. He is here for her, and now he is not even aware of her being around him. She leaves for home, but not without playing a prank on him.

She picks up a bit of sandal paste and with it, inscribes her message on Ratansen's chest, 'You don't know the art of begging; you were begging to see me and I came to you on my own but you had your eyes shut. Now, the moment has gone and you will have to strive hard to come to me.'

It is only after she leaves that the Gods in the temple come back to life.

But what about poor Ratansen?

Shiva and Parvati intervene

Coming out of his meditative state, Ratansen realizes the ironical prank fate has played on him. Padmavati came so close to him on her own, but...

All the conventional metaphors for the frustrated and suffering lover flow one after another in Jayasi's description of Ratansen's emotional turmoil. Ratansen recollects the separation stories of Shakuntala and Dushyant; Nala and Damyanti from the Mahabharata; and of Madhavanal and Kamkandla from *Simhasana Battisi* ('Thirty-two Tales of the Throne'). Thinking of Padmavati's prank, Ratansen says, 'Why did she choose sandal paste to inscribe her message on my chest? It had such a cooling effect on my burning heart and made me sleep.' But he

also experiences the heartburn of a missed opportunity. 'Tears of blood' is a well-known idiomatic expression of inconsolable grief and frustration; and 'Ratan' literally means jewel. Jayasi gives us the expression 'the jewel is crying, and tears of blood are dropping like rubies' (रोवै रतन लाल जनु चूरा।).

Ratansen takes out his frustration on God and calls the deity 'impure' (mlechcha). 'I have been worshipping you so that I can see her, and look what has come of it?' The poor deity replies apologetically, 'The moment she entered the temple my life was taken by Yama, and I don't know what happened after that. I am like a physician who is sick himself, how do I offer you any medication?'

With the deity also helpless, where is any hope for Ratansen? He must leave this world—dejected and defeated. Whether it's his own fault or a stroke of fate, he appears to have been rejected. (And who knew the pain of inexplicable rejection better than Jayasi?) Thus, Ratansen decides to end his failed life.

At the end of the epic, Padmavati along with Nagmati

commits sati at the pyre of Ratansen; but here in the middle, it is Ratansen who is going to commit sati. Jayasi was probably aware of the *Ishqnama* by Hasan Dilhawi mentioned at the beginning of this book. Possibly, other such legends were also in circulation in his time. In any case, for poets like Dilhawi and Jayasi, and more importantly, for their contemporary audience, sati was not the sole prerogative of women. It is not as if the modern editors or scholars have compared Ratansen's proposed act with sati. It is the poet himself: 'I could not get her by becoming a yogi and mendicant, now I will burn myself on a pyre like a sati' (पाएउँ नाहिं होइ जोगी जती। अब सर चढ़ौं जरौं असि सती)—204.

Undoubtedly, the idea of self-immolation is abhorrent, no matter who commits it. The point here, however, is that if at all it is to be treated as an expression of devotion and love, then why only women? Sometimes men also ought to be shown inclined towards it. Dilhawi and Jayasi do precisely that in their narratives.

Ratansen makes his own pyre but even before he can light it, the 'fire' emanating form Ratansen's suffering self makes everyone uncomfortable. Even Hanuman who had burned Ravana's Lanka cannot take the heat. He rushes directly to Shiva and tells him, 'Someone out there is burning everyone, even I am not able to withstand the burning sensation. If he actually lights the pyre, the entire world will be consumed by flames. Please intervene and do something.'

Shiva—in the guise of a leper—along with Parvati, appears at the scene. In the Hindu tradition, Parvati pleads on behalf of suffering souls. Shiva loves her too much to ignore her pleas, and helps, even if he is himself reluctant.

Shiva asks Ratansen not to commit the heinous act of self-immolation. He furiously shoots back, saying, 'Who is this trying to stop me? Don't you fear for your life? I am already half-burned; this pyre is only going to finish the job.' His voice emits so much heat and fire it is evident that without Mahadeva's intervention, the entire world would indeed be reduced to ashes. Parvati is impressed but still wants to test the depth of his love. She adopts the form of the most beautiful celestial apsara and tries to attract Ratansen, who does not show any interest. Parvati requests Shiva to help him. Seeing Mahadeva's reluctance, she vouches for Ratansen's 'truth', and reminds Shiva of the burden of two killings he has on his head; does he want to add the burden of a third now?

What Parvati is alluding to here are two famed incidents.

The first incident is when Shiva, due to his anger at being disturbed in his meditation, had killed Kamadeva—the God of love and desire. In the second incident, he had beheaded the clay-child created by Parvati to protect her privacy. In both the incidents, however, the victims were revived—the second as Ganesha.

Still, a killing is a killing, and Parvati is just cautioning her husband. Shiva, the doting husband, has never been able to ignore the pleas of his consort. How can he now?

In the meantime, Ratansen notices that the flies are not flying around the 'wounds' of this strange 'leper'; he is not even blinking his eyelids. His body does not cast any shadow either. He knows the truth now, and crying bitterly, he falls at Shiva's feet, 'O God of Gods, please help me.' Not just his eyes, but each and every pore of Ratansen's body overflows with tears; his cries fill the whole universe. Shiva consoles him and gives him the 'magic' (in the form of verbal instruction as well as a 'magic wand') to penetrate the impregnable fort of Simhal as well as his own self.

The trick, according to Jayasi's Shiva, is to recognize that, 'One is death as well as life. One is body as well as mind. One must act as if there is no other anywhere':

> (आपुहि मीचु जियन पुनि आपुहि तन मन सोइ ।
> आपुहि आपु करै जो चाहे कहाँ क दूसर कोइ ॥) —216

This is a typically mystic statement and is full of insight. No 'fort' can be entered without realizing one's true nature (potentials and limitations). There is an echo of the Bhagvad Gita here, 'One is one's own best friend and worst adversary.'

You have to first allow your potential self to enter and transform your present self. You have to transcend your limitations. This is the essence of any magic wand. The word used by Jayasi is siddhi i.e. mystical, miraculous achievement much more than mere magic.

The parrot saves the day

Ratansen now has the benefit of divine guidance and help. Using the magic trick granted to him, the 'army of yogis' surround the Simhal fort. The king sends his emissaries to enquire after the reason behind this strange siege. Ratansen explains, 'It is not a siege by aggressors. I am in fact only a beggar; I beseech his majesty to give me his daughter's hand in marriage and nothing else. Where else can a yogi go except the door which will bring him his siddhi?'

The emissaries are angry, 'How can a yogi or a beggar dare to ask for his majesty's daughter? Better run for your life before the king crushes you to dust. You talk of the princess's hand? All you are going to get here is a monkey's bite.'

A 'monkey's bite' is an allusion (testifying to the vastness of Jayasi's knowledge and the variety of his interests) to a popular story in which an impertinent yogi tricked a merchant into giving his daughter in service. The girl, however, was smart; she managed to replace herself with a ferocious monkey, and all the swindler 'yogi' got was a monkey-bite instead of the damsel's kiss. Ratansen's response to this allusion is firm and polite—'Even when bitten by a monkey or worse, a true yogi is not going to deviate from his path... My yoga is like water against which the fire of your king's anger won't be effective.'

King Gandharvsen, on hearing this response, gets angry, but decides to ignore the 'silly' yogi. Ratansen, on the other hand, cries out for Hiraman who, ever eager to help lovers in distress, immediately appears. Ratansen gives him a letter addressed to Padmavati. In the letter, he asks her to have faith in his truth, his love for her, and requests her to come to him. Hiraman promptly delivers the letter to its destination.

Jayasi, through Padmavati's response, takes the opportunity to once again underline the centrality of Padmavati in his narrative, and at the same time, place his epic in the tradition of similar love-narratives. Padmavati in her letter to Ratansen mentions categorically, 'You still have to prove that you deserve the honour of having me. You showed utter carelessness when I came to you. You claimed to meditate for me, but you did not even respond to my presence. In fact, you did not even act when I took the initiative of rubbing sandal paste on your chest. *You missed the opportunity of a lifetime, now you have to work hard all over again.'*

Here, a reference to famous love-narratives is made. Padmini asks, 'Remember how Vikram suffered for Swapnavati? He even went to paatal-lok (the netherworld of Nagas)... And the sufferings of lovers of *Madhumalati, Mrigavati* and *Premavati.* Also Aniruddha (Lord Krishna's son) who fought for Usha. Have you striven as hard as them? Have you taken enough pains? I also deeply love you, desire you, but you still have to prove your worth—do not forget, I am Padmavati, as distant as the seventh heaven; only he who is ready to eliminate himself will have my hand':

> (हौं रानी पदुमावति सात सरग पर बास।
> हाथ चढ़ौं सो तेहि कें प्रथम जो आपुहि नास॥) —233

The story of Vikramaditya and Swapnawati figures in the 'Thirty-two Stories of the Throne', and that of Aniruddha is from the Krishna Katha. *Madhumalati, Mrigavati* and *Premavati* are love-narratives composed in Awadhi by Sufi poets prior to Jayasi. Their popularity has been attested to in the seventeenth-century autobiography *Ardha Kathanak* (Half a Tale) of Banarasidas—the Jain merchant and founder of 'Adhyatama Panth'. By making his heroine refer to these works, Jayasi is paying tribute to his poetic ancestors and placing his own work in the same tradition.

Ratansen is excited and encouraged by Padmavati's reciprocation of his love and his siege of love continues with renewed determination. King Gandharvsen, irritated with the yogi's obstinacy, decides to finally act. The yogi and his companions are surrounded by the Simhal soldiers. Ratansen's companions, anticipating an assault, prepare themselves for an armed confrontation. Ratansen puts an end to it all. He says, 'We are not here to fight with arms. If it was possible to win love by force, why would so many siddhas (mystics), who knew the nature of love, sacrifice their lives? Our essence lies in our resolve of not using arms. Confronted with swords, let us be like water. Where is that sword which can cut through water?':

(जौं पै जाइ पेम सिउँ जूझा। कत तप मरहिं सिद्ध जिन्ह बूझा॥
यह सत बहुत जो जूझि न करिऐ। खरग देखि पानी होइ ढरिऐ॥
पानिहि काह खरग कै धारा। लौटि पानी होइ जो मारा॥) —243

Something very important and pertinent for lovers of all times is stated here. Ratansen, by sending a letter to Padmavati, has made sure that she reciprocates his feelings. It is not a one-way affair. Here, the poet recognizes a woman's individuality as a precondition for any attempt to 'impress' her. If she had not reciprocated and underlined her own initiative, perhaps, Ratansen would have perished in dejection; but the lover's siege of Simhal would certainly be lifted. He also knows force of arms and violence have no business in love, howsoever strong or 'true' your desire may be.

The core difference between Jayasi's Ratansen and Alauddin lies precisely here. Ratansen forbids the use of arms even when he has been assured of Padmavati's love for him while Alauddin couldn't care less. He just had to have Padmini even if it meant using deceit and brute force.

Irritated with Ratansen's stubbornness, the king orders his arrest. Padmavati comes to know of this intuitively and 'the lotus (Padma means lotus) fainted as soon as sun was eclipsed.' Everyone around grieves. Padmavati asks for Hiraman, 'Only he can help.' Hiraman is informed and rushes to Padmavati; he blesses her. She 'touches the parrot's feet' and forgetting all her ladylike reserve, she shares her plight with him, 'I love Ratansen. Please make us meet, just as the swan helped Damyanti (in the famous story from the Mahabharata) meet her separated husband.'

Hiraman is moved by her plight and her reverent dependence on him. He tells Padmavati, 'The problem is that your father loves his privileges as a king; he reveres Brahmins and gets yogis killed' (पिता तुम्हार राज कर भोगी। पूजै बिप्र मरावै जोगी ॥)—256.

These lines hint at the conflict between Brahmins and yogis in early modern India. Hearing this, the eclipse of the sun reaches the moon (Padmavati) as well. 'If that yogi dies, I am not going to live either. I will either serve him all his life or will depart from this world along with him. Hiraman, please teach me the art of entering the other body (Para-kaya-pravesh), so that I can enter him and die the moment he dies.'

Hiraman knows that 'true love transcends death' and tells Padmavati, 'As far as Ratansen is concerned, you are God. He has already achieved immortality due to your grace and love. Your eternal life has already entered him. Now, nobody, not even your father Gandharvsen can kill him.'

As the two friends are talking, Ratansen is being taken to be impaled on a suli (gibbet). Seeing his end, 'Mansur laughs.' We know of Mansur the Sufi who was executed for his love of God; here Ratansen is Mansur of Padmavati. When asked about his caste, Ratansen does not give the expected answer. He has gone beyond his socially ascribed identity. He is nothing but a man in love. In his own words, his caste is that of a yogi, of a 'beggar' of love.

Besides these two parallel scenes, a third one is also unfolding. A conscientious and fearless bard is trying to make King Gandharvsen withdraw his order. The most ironical thing about his request is the reference to Ratansen's virtual 'divinity'. The bard tells the king, 'You think he is an ordinary yogi? He is royal himself; anybody who looks carefully would know this. Moreover, he is aided by the gods. You harm him and you will have veritable Mahabharata at your doorstep. Shiva, Brahma, Indra, Sheshnaga, along with thirty-three crore gods, nine naths and eighty-four siddhas will rush to his help. Krishna himself will join in.'

The king is angry with the bard's impertinence, but is restrained by his advisers. The bard reminds the king of Hiraman who lived under his protection. He says, 'Why don't you send for him and verify whether I am right or wrong?'

The king remembers the past and regrets his ill treatment of Hiraman; but he is confident that, in spite of all that, Hiraman being a true pundit, a scholar, will not lie to him. He apologizes and requests Hiraman to tell the truth about the obstinate yogi. Hiraman does so; and that is how Ratansen's ordeal ends. His fortune turns and preparations for the royal wedding begin.

Two things are of utmost importance here. The divine help to challenge the king of Simhal and prevent a Mahabharata-like war is available to the love-yogi who is happily willing to die for his love. Nothing of that sort is available to the king of Chittor when confronted with Alauddin Khalji.

All the brilliant hyperbole used here is in fact for the glory of true love—royal or non-royal. It is not about the valour of a warrior, but that of a lover.

Secondly, Hiraman, a parrot, earns the confidence and respect of someone who wanted him dead. Contrast this with Raghav Chetan, another pundit, who brings calamity to the same woman who is generous and full of grace towards him. He is the only character in *Padmavat* without any redeeming human quality.

We will meet this perfidious pundit in due course.

Then they met...

Jayasi describes the royal wedding with delight. He celebrates various aspects of a householder's life. The description starts from the yogi Ratansen changing into the royal groom's attire. He must now discard the kantha (robe) made of chirkuts (small useless pieces of cloth) and put on golden garments studded with jewels. Chirkut is an expression very popular in north India, even today, as a metaphor for a worthless, idiotic person. Not only the religious rituals but also the social customs prevalent in Jayasi's time and place—many of which remain unchanged—are described with relish. The descriptions include huge feasts and sweet small talk between the bride's friends and the bridegroom. The poet also talks about the bride's paradoxical emotions—excited, expectant of the 'first meeting' and at the same time sad and anxious about the 'final separation' from her parental home and friends. Padmavati, to the surprise of her companions, is depressed at the sight of the wedding procession: 'This procession is going to take me away forever. I am never going to come back.'

This 'normal' emotion of South Asian brides becomes heart-wrenchingly true in her case.

The couple has been deep in love and has suffered a lot for each other; now is the moment of consummation. The description of this 'moment' and its aftermath runs into forty-two stanzas and is a mini masterpiece in itself.

Indian culture in Jayasi's times did not treat erotic desire and its expression as a sin. The Indian tradition considered kama (erotic desire) an integral part of a healthy life. Verbal or visual creative expressions of the erotic act and desire were not looked down upon. *The prudishness towards sex, which to some people's mind is the hallmark of Indian culture, is actually a 'gift' of the British Raj.* With colonialism came 'Victorian' prudishness and resistance to erotic expression in art and literature. Jayasi and his audience would find such rejection or suspicion not only not-Indian but quite foreign. They would judge any such description not on the touchstone of so-called 'obscenity', but on appropriate employment and competent handling.

Jayasi handles Eros (Kama) in a holistic way, with great sensitivity to both its physical and emotional aspects. He is clear that competence in erotic matters is a precondition for conjugal bliss and cannot be divorced from emotional aspect. Before proceeding to describe the consummation of the marriage, he once again underlines Padmavati's intellect through a sweet, suggestive exchange of witty remarks between her and her man. For the first time, we come to know that Ratansen, besides perseverance, possesses immense wit as well. There are remarks from Padmavati asking him to prove his worth and dependability; with inbuilt hints at events waiting in the wing—'One should fall in love only with someone consistent and belonging to one's own place. There is no point in being intimate with a yogi, a bumblebee and a foreigner'. To this, Ratansen responds with confidence, 'Listen, the truth is, I belong to you forever. I am one yogi who has already reached his destination. Borax once mixed with gold cannot be separated. The same is the case with us.'

The lover succeeds in convincing his beloved. One may add here that the poet succeeds in reiterating the couple's made-for-each-other status. The most moving, however, is the fact, that even in this intimate moment, Padmavati does not forget her debt to Hiraman. 'It was he who brought your message to me,' she fondly recalls.

It is only now that Jayasi proceeds to describing the actual erotic act; and that too, with great psychological insights. In his uninhibited rapturous description, Padmavati, even though knowledgeable of and competent in the erotic arts, is still apprehensive. She is willing, but cautious and shy. Ratansen—the lover who has been waiting for so long—is excited yet patient, forceful yet considerate.

The lovebirds continue to enjoy life. Jayasi demonstrates his mastery of yet another poetic convention—Shad-Ritu Varnan i.e. describing the six seasons from the lovers' point of view. Ratansen and Padmavati spend an entire year in fun, frolic, erotic and artistic enjoyments.

In Chittor, Nagmati cried through the year

To Jayasi, Nagmati is not merely a nagging wife or a symbol of worldly bonds. Just as Padmavati is not merely a stand-in for God or Ratansen for a devotee. In any case, it is not a good idea in fiction or in real life to reduce human beings into mere symbols of abstract ideas—good or bad.

Padmavat is not only about the grand love of Ratansen and Padmavati, but also the third person in this love triangle—its poor victim, Nagmati. As indicated earlier, it is through her that we get a sense of a woman's plight in a patriarchal system—irrespective of her status. Unlike Padmavati, she does not carry an aura of divinity around her. She is a queen, but in Jayasi's articulation of her suffering, Nagmati could be the woman next door.

It is important to note that Jayasi and his epic are products of their time. It would be anachronistic and futile to read any trace of 'feminism' in his treatment of Nagmati. Her world remains Ratansen-centric, in spite of all his insensitivity, and Jayasi describes her lamentations in an erotically suggestive, 'inviting' idiom, as was the poetic norm. The point, however, is the poet's awareness of the suffering of a woman whose husband discards her for no fault of her own.

Nagmati loves Ratansen and longs for him, while recognizing and being fully aware of her secondary status in his life (since he has heard of Padmavati). It is a year now since Ratansen has left for Simhal. Immediately after the Shad-Ritu Varnan of Ratansen and Padmavati, Jayasi turns to the grieving Nagmati's lamentations, creating an impactful contrast. He focuses solely on her for the next seventy-three stanzas, composed by following the poetic convention of Barahmasa (description of the past twelve months).

At the outset, there is a deliberate identification of Nagmati as an ordinary, rural woman as opposed to a privileged, urbane, sophisticated one: 'Nagmati waits in Chittor, watching the way expectantly for the lover who has not looked back. "He must have been enchanted by some city woman. That is why he ignores me"' (नागमती चितउर पँथ हेरा। पिउ जो गए फिरि कीन्ह न फेरा॥ नागरि नारि काहु बस परा। तेइँ बिमोहि मो सौं चितु हरा॥)—341.

We still have the memory (preserved in folk songs) of women from eastern Uttar Pradesh and Bihar cursing Kolkata (the first

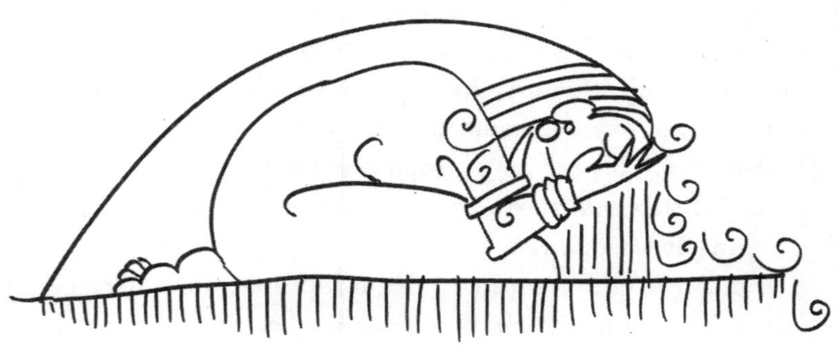

industrial centre to come up with the rise of British Raj) for having enchanted their men and holding them back. Many men from these areas left for Kolkata in search of employment and the pains of the women left behind found a voice in these folk songs. Jayasi's 'Nagmati Barahmasa', by blaming a 'city woman' for her suffering, implicitly puts Queen Nagmati in the company of such women who eagerly awaited the return of their men.

It is due to this 'universalization of sentiment' along with masterly employed poetic craft that this Barahmasa is considered 'one of the finest pieces of poetry' in Hindi literature.

It opens with mythological allusions in a typical Jayasi way. Nagmati blames Hiraman for depriving her of her husband, just as Vishnu in his Vaman avatar (incarnation as dwarf) had deprived King Bali of his kingdom, or as Akrur had taken away Krishna from the cowherd girls of Braj.

Nagmati's Barahmasa begins with the month of Ashaadh (late June–early July), when north India receives the first monsoon showers, and covers all the twelve months, describing the hues of her longing and pain in accordance with the change of season specific to each month. The beauty, however, lies in the fact that there is nothing specifically royal in these descriptions or in Nagmati's utterances. In one of them, she actually talks of the difficulties in mending the roof of her house (in fact, hut) all alone without his help. In her context, her words are not just true for royal women, but for any woman from any background: 'Blessed and proud are those women, whose husbands stay with them, the unfortunate ones like me can't even imagine happiness.'

Like any woman (or man for that matter), she wants to reach her beloved even if it means eliminating her existence. Recall

Ratansen's words for his beloved, at the beginning of this chapter, 'I want to turn into dust and reach her door...' Nagmati utters similar words for her husband, 'Let this body burn and turn into ash and let that fly with the wind so that it reaches the path traversed by my husband':

(यह तन जारौं छार कै कहौं कि पवन उड़ाउ।
मकु देहि मारग होइ परौं कंत धरै जहँ पाउ॥)

In this state of mind, she reaches the forest, leaving her palace behind, and a bird, moved by her plight, agrees to take her message to Ratansen. The bird flies to Simhal and reaches the forest where Ratansen is busy hunting. The bird delivers the message indirectly by telling the other birds of the 'strange king of Chittor who has insensitively left his wife, mother and kingdom for the love of a woman. Everybody there is in pain, his mother is almost dying and his wife is already half-dead; one doesn't know how a man can behave so irresponsibly and heartlessly'.

'I am that unfortunate king,' Ratansen cries out, 'I have been looking forward to some news from home, even though I left it as a yogi. Please tell me more...'

Jayasi introduces a wonderful wordplay (or shall we say 'idiom-play?) here in the bird's reply to Ratansen. It tells him, 'What yogi? You do not even know that the singi and conch-shell are held in the right hand, not in the left...'

The bird continues, pointing out the 'rightness' of rightward movement of many things. The wordplay here is on the association of 'good' deeds with the right hand. The 'right hand' in Hindi is seedha haath (सीधा हाथ), and in other contexts, seedha means 'simple and straight', as opposed to ulta (उलटा) which means 'crooked'. In English too, the word 'sinister' is etymologically connected with 'left-handed'.

The point this bird is making is also straight and simple: 'You did no good discarding your wife, mother and kingdom. In fact, you acted in a crooked manner.'

And it is here that Jayasi gives an emotional gloss to his own physical deformity: 'Muhammad says, since my beloved looked at me and spoke to me on my right side (rather in the 'right' way), I myself gave up my left eye and ear':

(मुहमद बाईं दिसि तजी एक सरवन एक आँखि।
जब ते दाहिन होइ मिला बोलु पपीहा पाँखि॥) —367

Simhal—the utopia, the island of Padmavati—is suddenly a foreign land to Ratansen. He experiences pangs of nostalgia for his own land. Padmavati's pleas to stay back in Simhal forever do not work. They have to move back to the reality of Chittor as soon as possible. For Ratansen, Padmavati at the moment symbolizes escape from reality into utopian. He needs to come back to the realities of life—his mother, the kingdom and Nagmati.

The last miracles

Ratansen seeks his father-in-law's permission to leave, saying it is not advisable for any king to leave his kingdom for such a long period. He repeats commonsensical statements like, 'Even brothers become mortal enemies for land and kingdom.' And it is here that for the first time in the epic, Delhi and its Sultan are mentioned, and with great concern: 'The Sultan of Delhi is quite near my place, if he rises (to take my kingdom) I will be like the moon at dawn' (उहाँ नियर ढीली सुलतानू । होइहि भोर उठिहि जौं भानु)—375.

Now, we are about to move from the utopian to the real. Supposedly, from 'imaginary' to 'historical'. It needs to be emphasized again that Jayasi is not writing history. In fact, his heart is not at all in historical or political descriptions, not even in the grandeur and conspiracies of the court. He is self-confessedly a poet of 'pain of love'; and his sole motivation for writing Padmavat *is simply to leave a 'mark on the memory'. The 'historical' is merely a medium for him to convey his articulation of 'pain of love' in an effective and relatable way. Looking for a narrative of history in his epic would have been incomprehensible or even amusing to Jayasi.*

Padmavat *is not part-imaginary and part-historical. It is a work of great creativity, employing a particular historical event for its purpose in an imaginative way.*

In this episode, Jayasi makes Padmavati foretell the chronicle of coming events in an ominous way; she tells her childhood friends, 'Let us embrace each other to our heart's contentment as I am leaving for the place from where there is no return' (मिलहु सखी हम तहँवा जाहीं । जहाँ जाइ फिर आवन नाहीं ॥)—379.

The people of Simhal bid the couple farewell with heavy hearts and in a fittingly royal manner; described with typical hyperbole.

Many ships are loaded with gifts for Ratansen and Padmavati. Everyone comes to see them off upto the seaport, wherefrom their beloved Padmavati has to negotiate the ocean (and life) with her husband. Henceforth, the poet notes, 'She has only her merits and demerits along with her, everyone else is left behind' (जौ पहुँचाइ फिरा सब कोऊ। चले साथ गुन औगुन दोऊ ॥)—385.

For the first time, the word 'demerit' is used with reference to Padmavati. She is leaving the unblemished innocence of utopia behind to enter the grey world of real relations and situations. The poet's statement is not just about her, but everyone's individual moral agency and accountability. Everybody reaches a point in life when s/he cannot depend on anything except their own merits and demerits. It is also a reminder of the inevitable existential fact that when a human leaves for the other world, no relative, friend or supporter accompanies him/her.

Beyond life, beyond your pyre or grave, it is only you and your karma.

Things do not go well for the couple despite all the astrological care that was taken before undertaking the voyage. Ratansen has a bout of pride at his newly-acquired dowry possessions from Simhal. 'In the whole world, who is going to match my riches now?' As if to put some sense in him and prepare him and the readers for the nature of things to come, there is a devastating sea storm and a swindling demon to torment him and his wife. Their fleet sinks, they are separated and without hope—they prepare to die.

But divine forces help them miraculously; this is the last entry of miraculous in the narrative. No miracles hereafter.

Ratansen is saved by Samudra (Lord of the ocean) and Padmavati by Lakshmi (Goddess of prosperity), consoling and inspiring the couple to move on. As if to compensate for the lost gifts, the divinities give them five invaluable gifts—nectar, a swan, a golden bird, a tiger cub and the philosopher's stone. Samudra also deputes some mermen to accompany them till the land. These mermen return when Ratansen and Padmavati are safely in Jagannath Puri (Odisha).

This is another clear hint that Jayasi's Simhal is located somewhere beyond Odisha.

They have reached Puri in penury. The five divine gifts are too divine to be of any practical use in human affairs. They don't even have money to buy boiled rice that is being sold near Jagannath Temple. The poet had mentioned at the beginning of the epic, 'The worth of anything is appreciated more by those deprived of it; those possessing it tend to take it for granted.' His hero now realizes that 'money makes you independent, hunger torments a poor man even more. A man without money is like a withered tree.'

Padmavati has some jewels which Goddess Lakshmi had secretly given her. It is by using them that they not only manage to obtain food, but also organize a small band of soldiers to accompany them to Chittor, where they are welcomed with great happiness, a grand celebration, and of course, Nagmati's jealousy.

So far so good, but isn't there something amiss here?

Hiraman has simply disappeared from the narrative. He is not seen even amongst those who came to see Padmavati and her husband off. Perhaps he was disappointed with Ratansen's resolve to go back; maybe he was heartbroken that his dearest friend Padmavati had to leave. Or probably he had had too much of human beings and was back to his own kind in the forest.

The poet gives no cause, but after this point, we never hear of Hiraman again; and Simhal is also referred to only at a few places.

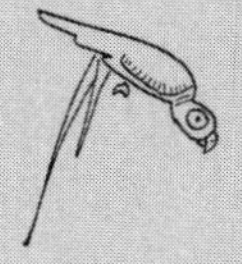

Chapter 4

Return to Reality

The wives' quarrel

Jayasi is mainly focused on exploring kama (erotic desire) in its many aspects, sometimes to the exclusion of other important situations. Describing Nagmati's grief, he had only fleetingly mentioned Ratansen's mother Saraswati; she was first mentioned when Ratansen was leaving for Simhal. But now when her son has come home, she simply disappears from the poet's compass while Nagmati's pleasure is noted in detail. Her 'burning jealousy' at the sight of Padmavati also gets due attention.

In a typical husbandlike manner, Ratansen assures his first wed of her superior status. She, however, knows the truth; but what can she do? She has to be happy with her Simhal-returned husband. But teasing sarcasm will do no harm. She compares her husband with an 'elephant who after a bath and a spread of sandal powder on his body will still put some dust on himself.'

The king handles his newly-wed wife in the same way—being his first wife, Nagmati is senior to Padmavati: 'But do I need to tell you, you are my life-breath.' Padmavati also has her armoury of sarcasm and insults, all directed at Nagmati, 'I know your "truth" my dear; but what can one do about a "body" which has been poisoned by a she-snake.'

Following the above separate dialogues between a husband and his two wives, we witness a proper quarrel between the wives. It starts in the palace garden and is ostensibly a discussion about flower-plants, their characteristics and maintenance. Each sentence is loaded with double meaning—working simultaneously

for or against one of the quarrelling duo. Soon, the dialogue degenerates into a full-fledged fist fight and hair-pulling. They fight like 'drugged ones, no one dares to separate them'.

Ratansen rushes to the scene and tries to pacify the fighting women—both are valuable to him, he cannot afford to lose either woman. It is important to note here that Jayasi's Ratansen has no other woman in his life except these two. Jayasi has thus made Ratansen's love for both the women in his life seem quite credible.

The poet shows his hero free of the 'royal' habit of treating women as nothing more than sex objects and also saves him from the emotionally devastating choice of choosing one over the other. He inserts his own signature in Ratansen's plea to them, 'Muhammad says, it is destined (by God or maybe even by poet Muhammad himself) for you both to live tougher like Ganga and Yamuna, enjoy life and serve (your husband)':

(तुम्ह गंगा जमुना दुइ नारी लिखा मुहम्मद जोग।
सेव करहु मिलि दुनहूँ औ मानहु सुख भोग॥) —445

In any case, the quarrelling wives hardly have any other choice except to accommodate each other. Given the general temper of the times, Ratansen not having a third one to make this choice is somewhat reassuring and more than a mere compulsion.

Had Jayasi been a 'modern' poet, these two women would have reflected on their condition and on the difference in the way a man and a woman looks at love! He was not that modern, but was still 'early modern' enough to ensure that Ratansen was in a serious relationship with only these two.

The three of them, it seems, could have lived happily ever after, but for...

Raghav Chetan: The perfidious pundit

Jayasi at this point seems to be in a hurry to be done with his epic. As soon as the narrative moves from Simhal to Chittor, its structure starts getting disjointed. Raghav Chetan, the perfidious pundit appears out of the blue to act as fate's instrument of devastation. He is a scholar, an astrologer and also commands a yakshini (female member of an ethereal species with ambiguous ethical temperament) who helps him create illusions. In other words, he knows the 'science' of individual and mass hypnosis.

Jayasi introduces this character with a tongue-in-cheek remark: 'He was "too intelligent"' (राघव चेतनि चेतनि महा…)—446.

Once, on a new moon day, the king asks, 'What is the tithi (date in lunar calendar) today? 'It is doej (second),' Raghav Chetan responds with careless confidence. The other pundits are shocked and insist, 'Today is amavasya (new moon), doej will only be two nights later.'

It becomes an issue of prestige and soon there is a wager that the losing party will be banished from the country. When the evening dawns, with the help of yakshini, Raghav Chetan creates a mass hypnosis and everybody sees the moon in its doej form. But the next night—the first night after the new moon—the pundits point out to the king that the size of the moon has decreased as compared to last night which was shown as that of doej. The king realizes that he has been taken for a ride. On the 'touchstone of logic', once again it is proven that 'all that glitters is not gold'.

The king contemplates ordering the charlatan's execution, but considering his Brahmin birth only banishes him.

The poet here takes us in Raghav Chetan's skin. He knows things academically, but has no moral integrity, which is a fundamental requirement of a genuine scholar. Instead of feeling ashamed of his cheating act, he goes into a rant of self-righteous anger, 'I served this miserable king who does not value scholars.'

As indicated earlier in this book, Raghav Chetan, the Brahmin scholar, is the only major character in *Padmavat* without any redeeming quality at all. His name underlines the irony dramatically. 'Raghav' (a descendent of the Raghu clan) is usually used for Ram; and Chetan means 'aware'. This character has neither the idealism of Ram nor basic ethical awareness. He bites the hand that feeds him; all his acts are motivated by baser instincts and negative intent.

Padmavati comes to know of the banishment of the 'guni' (which literally means qualified, but here it is being used for her apprehension about Raghav Chetan's character) Brahmin and gets worried. Here, we see her pragmatic side, 'The king did not act wisely. One who can show doej on a new moon night with a yakshini's help can some day show the moon facing the sun as well (i.e. can bring unthinkable disaster). Moreover, he is a poet as well, and a poet's tongue is like a double-edged sword; it carries water on one side and fire on the other (i.e. a poet's speech can cause both strife and reconciliation.) What if he goes out talking bad things about the king? One earns reputation with very hard work, but can lose it with the slightest indiscretion.'

(कै गियान धनि अगम बिचारा। भल न कीन्ह अस गुनी निसारा॥
जेइँ जाखिनी पूजि ससि काढ़ी। सुरुज के ठाउँ करै पुनि ठाढ़ी॥
कबि के जीभ खरग हिरवानी। एक दिसि आग दोसर दिसि पानी॥
जनि अजगुत काढै मुख भौरें। जस बहुतें अपजस होइ थोरें॥)—450

Thinking well of her husband, Padmavati wants to pacify Raghav Chetan; she calls him to her quarters. He comes under her balcony and merely takes a fleeting glance at her, as she gives away one of her priceless bangles as a gift to him. This fleeting glance is enough to make Raghav Chetan unconscious. Seeing once again the impact of her beauty, Padmavati laughs slightly and leaves the scene. Raghav Chetan is brought to his senses by his attendants, and the first thought to cross his mind is to somehow get another similar bangle. 'That should be enough to take care of my whole life,' he reasons and decides there and then to go to Alauddin—the 'Turk' Sultan of Delhi, 'famous for his Alai dinars (coins of authentically purified gold).' 'He is bound to give me another bangle of this type if I tell him about this lotus (Padmavati). After knowing about her, he will rise on Chittor as the sun rises in the sky, and under its heat, I will watch Ratansen palpitate like a fish in sand.'

He immediately leaves for Delhi, reaches the royal palace, presents himself as a Brahmin beggar and waits for an audience with the Sultan.

Jayasi had gone into raptures while singing of the transformative impact of Padmavati's beauty. Her beauty is so pristine that it takes away the sins, and sends people into a trance. By making Raghav Chetan immune to this transformative impact, the poet is making another important point. The paras (philosopher's stone) has transformative power, but it doesn't work on other stones, but only on iron. You have to have some potential for transformation. Raghav Chetan lacks even that.

Moreover, we are in the real world now, far away from the utopia of Simhal.

Apart from the utter depravity of Raghav Chetan's mind, the other notable fact is that in this part of the epic, which is a narrative of harsh realities, he is the only one with any 'miracle abilities'.

The message is clear. In real life, there are hardly any miracles, except those of the human spirit—courage and other human qualities. It is wise to look at all other miracle claims with a healthy suspicion.

Enter Alauddin

In his exploration of erotic desire, Jayasi makes Alauddin Khalji represent a particular aspect of male desire. Just like Ratansen, Alauddin also gets obsessed with Padmini after hearing about her unparalleled beauty. The difference, however, is that he wants to have her with brute force. Ratansen transformed himself into a 'beggar of love' to reach Padmavati and took pains to convince her of the sincerity of his dedication. He won her heart before having her; went to the extent of almost committing 'sati', even faced probable execution. Alauddin shows no such inclination towards self-sacrifice. He is not at all bothered about her willingness. For him, she is not a person, but just another likely possession, another (potential) proof of his prowess.

In Jayasi's treatment, Alauddin's desire is undoubtedly unjust. He is certainly insensitive to Padmavati as an individual and is aggressively assertive, also cunning; and yet, Jayasi's Alauddin is not just a monster. Along with demerits, he also has merits. As a ruler, he is competent and careful of the welfare of his subjects, irrespective of caste and creed. While giving alms, he does not differentiate on the basis of religion. He presides over an expansive empire, as if carrying the 'load of the whole universe' on his shoulders and controls an intricate intelligence network required for such an empire. In Jayasi's poetic hyperbole, Alauddin 'had his eyes everywhere on earth and sky... How can a king effectively rule, if he is not this careful and cognizant?'

These descriptions are quite in consonance with the historical Alauddin Khalji, and that makes his character in *Padmavat* credible.

But there is more to it. Being a character in an epic composed by a great poet, Alauddin in *Padmavat* is also capable of existential reflections on the vagaries of life and transience of political power. Most importantly, let us recall once again the words of Vasudeva Sharan Agrawal—'A little Ram Katha can be carved out of *Padmavat*.' The idiom of Alauddin's reflections in *Padmavat* too is coloured by Ram Katha.

Jayasi describes him receiving the news of a 'strange beggar' at his door in the following words:

'The Shah took mercy the moment he heard of the strange beggar and ordered, "Ask him about the route he took. After all, one day all of us have to take a route (to the other world); it is better to know it beforehand."'

The king was also concerned about Dhilli (Delhi)—'You have to attentively churn (the political power) to reach and retain its essence. You cannot be too careful in this regard, you cannot allow Dhilli to be Dheeli (i.e. loose, a wordplay—you cannot loosen your grip on political power). So many proud kings of Dhilli have been reduced to dust. Dhilli will exist only as long as it is prosperous, i.e. as long as the courtiers and people are happy. (If one does not take care of all this, then, remember, *Lanka of Ravana was burned and people warmed their hands in this heat; no youth and no pleasures were left in Lanka.*) One should give alms to every beggar, whether he is a Brahmin or a bard.'

As ordered, the beggar is presented and he pays his respects by touching the ground with his head.

(मया साहि मन सुनत भिखारी। परदेसी कहँ पूंछु हकारी॥
हम पुनि है जाना परदेसा। कौनु पंथ गवनब केहि भेसा॥
ढीली राज चिंत मन गाढ़ी। यह जग जैस दूध महँ साढ़ी॥
सैति बिरोरि छाँछि कै फेरा। मथि घिउ लीन्ह महिउ केहि केरा॥
एहि ढीली कत होइ होइ गए। कै कै गरब छार सब भए॥
तेहि ढीली का रहि ढिलाई। साढ़ी गाढ़ि ढीलि जब ताई॥
रावन लंक जारि सब तापा। रहा न जोबन औ तरुनापा॥
भीखि भिखारहिं दीजिऐ का बाभनु का भाट।
अग्याँ भई हँकारह धरती धरै लिलाट॥) —459

Raghav Chetan comes to his point straightaway. After all, he is here not to seek alms, but to destroy the woman who has been so generous to him. He tells Alauddin about her. The Sultan dismisses his description of Padmavati with disbelief and says, 'I have many padminis in my palace.' The perfidious pundit does not give up so easily. Realizing that the Sultan is treating him as just an ordinary beggar, he seeks to establish his credentials as a 'wide-ranging scholar'. He also claims to be worldly-wise, having seen all the 'seven islands'. 'I am not telling any lies,' he says, 'I, a begging Brahmin, am here in the presence of the most powerful king—your majesty rules in accordance with dharma. All the royal families respect you. How dare I speak a lie to you?'

Having thus made the Sultan interested, Raghav Chetan proceeds first to describe the four types of women elaborated in erotic science. After establishing his credentials as a 'scholar'; he comes to Padmavati: 'This woman, belonging to the padmini type, brought from Simhal, has a body like that of the purest gold and has the fragrance of a lotus. In fact, I can't describe her as she is beyond any verbal and visual descriptions by poets and painters.' As expected, this description runs into several stanzas, and like the one by Hiraman to Ratansen, it mentions her intellectual competence as well.

Raghav Chetan also informs Alauddin about the five invaluable gifts Ratansen received from Samudra and Lakshmi. 'Even Alexander did not possess such rarities,' he says, 'along with Padmavati, they too must be possessed by you.'

Alauddin fancied himself as the Alexander of his times. He was referred to as Sikandar Sani (Alexander The Second) in coin inscriptions and official prayers. He must possess rarities not possessed even by Alexander The First.

He not only handsomely rewards Raghav Chetan, but also promises to put him on the throne of Chittor. Raghav Chetan, in any case, has already gotten his reward. His baser instinct of 'revenge' initiates a turn of events which is going to end only with Padmavati—the epitome of beauty, along with her dedicated lover, and her rival in love (Nagmati)—being reduced to a handful of dust and ashes.

There are people in all times, in all societies, who out of sheer pettiness deliberately conspire to destroy beauty and love. Through Raghav Chetan, Jayasi's Padmavat *warns us against such depraved characters.*

The battle at Chittor

Alauddin sends 'advice' to Ratansen through his emissary Sarja, asking him to hand over Padmini of Simhal along with the five gifts of Samudra and Lakshmi. Ratansen furiously asks Sarja to behave himself. Sarja tries to lure him, 'The Sultan will give you the charge of Chanderi (a small town in present Madhya Pradesh), accept the offer; why bother so much for Padmini—a slave?' (उपर लेहि चँदेरी का पदुमिनि एक दासि)—490.

Ratansen's response to this insulting 'offer' is not merely a proud king's response, but also that of any self-respecting householder's, 'Your master may be the emperor, but every man's home is his own palace' (मँदिर एक कहूँ आपन साजू).

The implication of the statement is obvious and it is not meant only for Alauddin but for every ruler—'the sanctity of every household must be respected.'

Ratansen further adds, 'What value will Chanderi or even Chittor have if I have to suffer the humiliation of parting with the lady of my house? Every man, except a yogi, lives because of his love for his home...(and as far as Padmavati is concerned) I showed determination like that of Vikramaditya and won over

Simhal (got her), and your emperor thinks he can force his wish on a lion like me? He seems to have a petty mind (unexpected of a great emperor) to write such a letter':

(जौं पैं ग्रिहिनि जाइ घर केरी। का चितउर केहि काज चँदेरी॥
जिऐं लेइ घर कारन कोई। सो घऱ देइ जो जोगी होई॥

विक्रम सरिस कीन्ह जेइँ साका। सिंघल दीप लीन्ह जौं ताका॥
ताहि सिँघ कै गहै को मोंछा। जौं अस लिखा होइ नहिं ओछा॥) —491

He also throws a challenge of competing in love and determination to Sarja's master, 'If he really wants to have a padmini woman, he should go to Simhal himself' (चाहै नारि पदुमिनी तौ सिंघल दीपहि जाउ).

The poet could not have highlighted the difference between Ratansen and Alauddin's desire in bolder relief. Both men are 'obsessed' with the most beautiful woman. One of them performed a sadhana, underwent a lot of sufferings, ensured the consent of the woman he desires; and inspite of being a warrior never thought of using arms in his efforts for her. The other one does not bother about seeking the consent of the woman concerned. He cannot imagine any 'method' of love except that of brute force and aggression. Even his emissary refers to the woman in question as a slave.

Unimpressed with Ratansen's reasoned response, Sarja persists in his lord's demand and dismisses Ratansen's challenge derisively, 'Padminis from Simhal come to my lord on their own. What is Simhal for him, whom the whole world serves?'

It is at this point, that Chhitai—princess of Devgiri—is mentioned. 'The Sultan wanted and had her,' declares Sarja with swagger. We have briefly discussed *Chhitai Charit* in the first chapter; here in Sarja's boast, we see no hint of Alauddin's humane portrayal found in that text.

Now, Ratansen is left with no choice, but to accept the challenge. Sarja too reports back to Alauddin. A war is inevitable. Both sides prepare and as expected, the poet uses hyperbole with relish along with his usual display of knowledge. This time we are treated to a description of twenty-five breeds of horses. Later on, while describing the battle, he will give details of weaponry and war manoeuvres.

The Sultan sends messages to all his vassals to join the campaign against Chittor. The impact of his decision to attack Chittor is described with the usual hyperbole. The earth, as we know, is carried by Sheshnaga on his head, who himself is sitting on a tortoise. The tortoise, leaving his characteristic slumber, is fidgeting, the ocean is churning; there is variable earthquake. Such is the impact of Alauddin's preparations.

Hyperboles are integral to the poetic idiom of Jayasi and his contemporaries. What is remarkable is the spontaneous overflow of metaphors and allusions from Hindu mythology in Jayasi's mind.

On Alauddin's side, all his warriors won't be Muslims (or 'Turks' in Jayasi's own idiom). He will have fighters from the entire length and breadth of India.

Jayasi like many of his contemporaries had a clear geographical sense of India, which is expressed here and at other places through the phrase—from Himalayas in north to the ocean in south; from Ghazni (in present-day Afghanistan) in the west to Gaur (Bengal) in the east' (हेम सेत, गौर गजना).

In Jayasi's poetic 'report', Alauddin's army has vassals (amongst many others) from Kashmir, Odisha, Bengal and Sindh, even from Kamrup (present-day Assam) and Rameshwaram. Not only India, even the sultans of Rume (Constantinople) and Sam (Syria) have not stayed back! (रहा न रूम साम सुलतानू।)

The centrality of Chittor to Hindu kings (from Rajasthan, as many Hindu kings from other parts are described as joining Alauddin) is underlined here. We are informed that Alauddin's Hindu vassals, 'hearing his campaign against Chittor', collectively met to tell him: 'Chittor is like mother to all Hindus, in adverse times, one doesn't snap relations with one's mother. Ratansen has undertaken a jauhar, he is a respected Hindu king. Hindus have destiny like that of moths, and (for Chittor's defence), we would rush like moths rushing to fire. You please either be like the pleasant wind (i.e. drop the idea of invading Chittor), or happily give us the paan ka bida i.e. allow us to do the honourable thing and die in its defence. Bid us farewell.'

'Hearing this, Alauddin smiled good-humouredly. He bade

them farewell, saying, "You can decide in three days. In any case, who can help those who are bent upon burning themselves in fire?"'

(करत जो राय साहि के सेवा। तिन्ह कहँ पुनि अस आउ परेवा॥
सब होइ एकहि मतें सिधारै। पातसाहि कहँ आइ जोहारै॥
चितउर है हिंदुन्ह कै माता। गाढ़ परैं तजि जाइ न नाता॥
रतनसेनि है जौहर साजा। हिंदुइ माँह अहै बड़ राजा॥
हिंदुन्ह केर पनिंग कर लेखा। दौरे परहिं आगि जहँ देखा।
किरिपा करसि त करसि समीरा। नाहिं त हमहिं देहि हँसि बीरा॥
हम पुनि जाइ मरहिं ओहि ठाऊँ। मेटि न जाइ लाज कर नाऊँ॥
दीन्ह साहि हँसि बीरा आवहिं तीन दिन बीच।
तिन्ह सीतल को राखे आगि जिन्हें आगि महँ मीच॥) —502

Paan ka bida literally means a properly folded betel leaf (primarily with betel nut, lime, catechu and many other ingredients according to taste). In India, it serves as a metaphor (depending upon the context) of showing respect and regard, giving and accepting a challenging responsibility and respectful farewell. Alauddin's Rajput vassals are requesting him to allow them to leave with mutual respect. Alauddin on his part is mature enough to appreciate their emotional state and clear enough of his own goal. Both parties will face each other in the battle as honourable adversaries. None is either cowardly or monstrous.

Here, for the first time, the term jauhar occurs. It is being used to underline the determination of Ratansen and his people to fight till the last breath.

Jauhar refers to the Rajput custom of women committing collective self-immolation in a sieged fort, after all the men have left for the final battle with absolutely no hope of return.

It was seen as the last desperate step against any invader. Most importantly, it was *not* a Hindu custom, but only specific to Rajputs. Other Hindu warrior communities like the Marathas or Jats rarely showed any inclination towards it. In our times, we need to take it just as a fact of history of a particular region. Glorifying jauhar in whatever way—verbal or visual—just caters to the male chauvinistic fantasy of total control of women and the total surrender on her part. Glorification of such fantasies is co-terminus with the denial of human individuality to half of humanity—hence it is inhuman in itself.

But it is also senseless anachronism to judge the historical actors by our contemporary ethical standards, without any sensitivity to their context.

From this point of view, it is indeed remarkable that Jayasi's writing in the sixteenth century about a fourteenth-century event just 'factually informs' the readers of jauhar at the very end of the epic. Far from any glorification or celebration, he gives exactly three words to report the jauhar of Chittor.

Ratansen is also gathering allies and forces. Along with the aforementioned kings who inform the Sultan of their decision of siding with Ratansen, there are many warlords and warriors who join Ratansen. Tomars, Parmars, Baghelas, Chauhans, Chandels and many more decide to fight on his side. The most interesting in this list is the mention of Khatris and Agarwars. Khatris is a well-known, prosperous, trading caste mainly from Punjab. One is not sure, if the term 'Agarwars' is used for Agrawals, another trading caste, which believes in its 'Kshatriya origins'. In any case, it is another hint of the dynamism of professions and social roles of various castes in early modern India.

Read with care, Padmavat *and other such works can help*

greatly in the much-needed relook at the history of India before the British Raj.

Quite understandably, the size of Ratansen's allies and level of his preparations is no match to those of Alauddin's. *Most significantly, on Ratansen's side, there is absolutely no mention of Simhal and its king, Gandharvsen—his father-in-law.*

Jayasi, given to enthusiastic use of poetic hyperbole (and appreciated for his liberal use of metaphors and allusions), is careful of not using the fabulous utopia of Simhal even as part of hyperbole at this moment. Simhal is not only beyond the real world, it is now beyond even the poetic licence. Only the elephants from Simhal are mentioned as part of Ratansen's army. Also, there is absolutely no hint of the divine help Ratansen was assured when he was faced with the possibility of being executed in Simhal for loving Padmavati.

That was Simhal; this is Chittor. That was a love-yogi's struggle for his love; this is a husband's struggle for his wife, a king's struggle for his reign. That was the utopia of fables; this is a kingdom in reality. No scope of miracles and divinity exists here.

Jayasi puts Ratansen in a 'do *and* die' situation most succinctly. He knows the superior strength of the adversary and tells his warriors, 'Whatever could be done, we have done; now we have to just fight and die':

(राजैं कहा कीन्ह सौ करना। भएउ असूझ सूझ जस मरना॥) —512

His words reflect his acceptance of harsh reality along with his heroic spirit.

The battle scenes are described in great detail. There is a lot of information about weapons, ranging from swords to field guns.

We are also informed of Alauddin's army having Syrian, African, even firangi (most probably Portuguese) soldiers and mercenaries. Following the poetic conventions of the times, the poet describes the demonic beings feasting, even organizing their 'wedding ceremonies as the flesh of slain warriors is abundantly available' (अनँद बियाह करहिं मँसुखाए। अब भख जरम जरम कहँ पाए). 'Those who ate others (i.e. animals) are being eaten up now'—the poet notes ironically and comes to a philosophical conclusion—'Nobody takes the body along (to the other world), even though everybody seeks to make it healthy and sound, but how sound it has actually become can be judged only when it is weighed i.e. when one's contribution is assessed':

(काहूँ साथ न तनु गा सकति मुऐ पै पोखि।
ओछ पूर तब जानब जब भरि आउब जोखि॥) —519

Inspite of the disadvantage of fighting from within the fort with his resources and army being of no match to that of Alauddin's, Ratansen's personal bravery and battle skills are absolutely matchless. This fact comes out clearly again and again in the details of the one-to-one confrontations and of the battle in general. Speaking of this over several stanzas, Jayasi sums it up most succinctly and poetically in a couplet: 'The Shah's army attacked from all the four directions, the fort was surrounded by fire, the sun had eclipsed the moon, which in its turn became Rahu to eclipse the sun.'

(लागि कटक चारिहु दिसि गढ़ सो परा अगिडाहु।
सुरुज गहन भा चाँदहि चाँद भएउँ जस राहु॥) —522

Jayasi has generally compared Ratansen with the moon, here Alauddin is like the sun, eclipsing the moon, but Ratansen is also eclipsing him, just as Rahu (an asura in Hindu mythology) eclipses the sun.

With all his enthusiasm for Ratansen's character, Jayasi is 'realistic' enough not to ignore the difference between his military resources and strength and that of Alauddin's. This realistic awareness underscores his description of battle scenes. Moreover, for him, being morally sympathetic to Ratansen does not mean portraying Alauddin in a completely negative light. This makes Jayasi's *Padmavat* much more impactful than any opulent and flat retelling of the 'Padmini of Chittor' story.

Alauddin's siege continues for 'eight years'. According to the chronicles, however, it was only a matter of eight months—January to August 1303! Alauddin did not want to break down the fort with force, as he knew this would lead to jauhar and his desire for Padmini would remain unfulfilled. In the meanwhile, disturbing news begins to arrive from Delhi. This is not merely a poetic hyperbole. By the later part of 1303, there were Mongol disturbances which posed a serious threat to the Delhi Sultanate. Mongols were the most ferocious warriors in the thirteenth-fourteenth centuries and were feared for the utter destruction they brought to any land they attacked. They started invading India in 1297 and were a constant threat to the sultanate. The Mongol invasion in 1303, when Alauddin was busy with his Chittor campaign, was the most ferocious and serious. With great determination and leadership skills, Alauddin succeeded in warding off the Mongol invasions of India.

This particular moment in *Padmavat* serves very well as an example for the general point this book is trying to make. Here is an interesting mix of poetic imagination and historical fact. The siege having lasted for eight years is simply a hyperbole, but within this hyperbolic context, the 'disturbing news from Delhi' refers to an actual historical fact. And so, in the overall structure of the epic, the central character Padmavati is 'more than real', while the battle is a historical fact.

It needs to be reiterated that although we get many insights into the society and culture of the time from *Padmavat* and other such texts, it is futile, rather counterproductive, to read them as proper history; and debate the historicity of each and every event and character. It is even worse to assume that Jayasi and other poets had no knowledge of history. We should realize that an epic like *Padmavat* cannot be written without deep roots in tradition and knowledge of the past and present. But it still remains a work of creative imagination, not a 'factual' record or report.

Coming back to the narrative, Alauddin is concerned about the reports he is receiving—the siege of Chittor is not tenable. He must return to Delhi soon. He has to act single-mindedly. 'The mind thinking of one thing and acting on another is not a healthy mind,' the Sultan tells himself and takes a conscious decision to defeat Ratansen by deceit. He will be won over 'by giving paan ka bida [by showing regard and respect], as otherwise he is too hard a nut to crack' (पाहन कर रिपु पाहन हीरा। बेधौं रतनसेन पान दै बीरा॥)—533.

The treacherous truce

Having made up his mind, Alauddin sends Sarja to Ratansen to repeat his earlier offer with a crucial amendment. Now Ratansen is required to hand over the five invaluable gifts Samudra had given him. As a return gift, he will be given Chanderi Fort along with the Sultan's protection as the ruler of Chittor. Sarja conveys the offer to Ratansen, along with the warning, 'You have been entrapped like a bird in a cage, be sensible or it is just a matter of days before your fort is broken down. You will meet Hamir's fate.'

Hamir, the ruler of Ranthambore, had been vanquished by Alauddin only a couple of years before.

Ratansen meets bravado with bravado, 'Hamir lived up to and died for his decision; I will do the same. In fact, I am braver and stronger than him. I have supplies reserved for sixty years and sixteen lakhs soldiers, battle-ready! I am determined to commit jauhar.'

Incidentally, a gentle reminder to those who try to read imaginative literature dryly like realistic official documents and records; both sixty years and sixteen lakhs are poetically hyperbolic figures conveying an emotion, not a fact. You find many grandiose statements like this not only in *Padmavat*, but in many premodern epics around the world.

With all the bravado, both sides have their reasons to be realistic and seek an early end to hostilities. In response to Sarja's further talk, which is much softened, Ratansen is also disarming, 'After all, Sarja, who can deny the fact that emperor is revered by us all?' (अनु सरजा को मेंटै पारा। पातसाहि बड़ आहि हमारा ॥)—537.

The offer of a truce is accepted, and the emissaries from Chittor immediately leave for Alauddin's camp with Samudra's 'invaluable five'—swan, golden bird, nectar, tiger and the philosopher's stone. The emperor expresses his wish to visit Chittor the very next day, and the king orders a big feast in his guest's honour.

Jayasi had described another feast before this one—the wedding feast in Simhal; but the description of this feast surpasses that one by many degrees. It is not just a poet's description but that of a chef. Jayasi goes into meticulous details of the preparations and cooking—choosing the right kind of animals, fish, vegetables and a variety of grains—particularly rice; cutting and cleaning of fish, meat and vegetables; ensuring the right warmth of cooking-fire and the right quantity. Incidentally, the potato—the most ubiquitous Indian vegetable today—finds no mention for the simple reason that it arrived in India centuries after Jayasi.

The names of dishes prepared for the feast run into the dozens, and the cooking of each is explained with great care. The desserts and beverages (strictly non-alcoholic), even the betel leaves served at the end, are given similar meticulous attention. I am not competent enough to comment on the accuracy or lack thereof in these descriptions, but going by the relish with which Jayasi has described the feast, it seems he was not merely a foodie, but a master chef himself.

But quite the opposite may also be true. Jayasi was a poet with a scholar's inquisitiveness. Remember, he has been called 'the researcher of Indian Truth'. And for a genuine researcher the truth is not confined to merely esoteric and spiritual matters. It is quite possible that far from being a foodie or a chef himself, he painstakingly gathered relevant information to make his poetic utterances credible and sound. This could be true not only of food but of his other descriptions as well. Whatever is the case, at the end of it all, Jayasi comes back to his poet avatar, and philosophizes poignantly: 'All the dishes described hitherto, could come to existence only after getting a touch of water. If you examine carefully, all taste depends on water. There is no nectar but water. It holds the life in the body. Milk and ghee are but forms of water. If the body loses water, it also loses life-breath. It is water that holds light; rubies and pearls are found in water. Water is unblemished, its touch takes any scum away. And, yet, with all these qualities, water flows down politely, instead of nurturing highbrow haughtiness. Says Muhammad, deep waters, not shallow ones reach the ocean. Fulfilled (people and vessels) maintain equanimity, while the empty ones make a lot of noise.'

(जाति परकार रसोइँ बखानी। तब भइ जब पानी सों सानी॥
पानी मूल परेखौ कोई। पानी बिना सवाद न होई॥
अंब्रित पानि न अंब्रित आना। पानी सों घट रहै पराना॥
पानि दूध महँ पानी घीऊ। पानि घटैं घट रहै न जीऊ॥
पानि दूध महँ पानी घीऊ। पानि घटैं घट न रहै जीऊ॥
पानी माहँ समानी जोती। पानिहि उपजै मानिक मोंती॥
पानी सब महँ निरमरि करा। पानि जो छुवै होइ निरमरा॥
सो पानी मन गरब न करई। सीस नाइ खाले कहँ ढरई॥
मुहमद नीर गँभीर जो सो नै मिलै न समुँद।
भरे ते भारी होइ रहे छूंछे बाजहिं दुँद॥) —551

The importance of water, not only for human life but for existence as such, can never be overemphasized. The poet's brilliance lies in the context he chooses to highlight this. *A lesser poet, while describing the preparations for such a grand feast would perhaps take water for granted. Jayasi is a great poet, and knows the crucial importance of not only water, but also of other things which are generally taken for granted. From him, we can learn to be more attentive and sensitive to people, things, spaces and practices we have gotten used to taking for granted; for example, tolerance in personal, social and political spheres.*

The evocative value of this stanza can be better appreciated by those who have a sense of the Hindi/Urdu idiom. Pani or water is a metaphor for the honour and worth of a human being and the 'shine' of an object. A very famous couplet by Rahim (a high-ranking official and general in Akbar's court and a Hindi poet greatly respected for his ethical aphorisms) puts it succinctly: 'One should always be careful to preserve one's pani; if it is gone, a human being is of no value, as is the case with a pearl (without its hue) or dough (without the right amount of water in it):

(रहिमन पानी राखिए, बिन पानी सब सून।
पानी गये न ऊबरे मोती, मानस, चून॥)

Alauddin arrives the next day and is given a tour of the fort. Apart from the details and metaphors characteristic of his descriptions, Jayasi creates a most significant scene—describing the great surprise that Alauddin experiences. He is taken to a high point of the fort for a bird's-eye view of the city. Apart from a city as beautiful as 'Indra puri, full of waterbodies, gardens, attractively decorated houses', he sees hale and hearty people going about their businesses, even playing games; simply enjoying life as normally, in fact, as pleasantly 'as if the fort has never been surrounded' (चैन चाउ तस देखा जनु गढ़ छेका नाहिं) —554.

Even under siege, Chittor is an adequately fortified and battle-ready community, not a depressingly militarized one. If one needs to glorify something at all, it should be this facet of Chittor's life as imagined by Jayasi, not the custom of jauhar.

Moving around the palace, Alauddin's only thought is Padmavati. Jayasi describes his inner thoughts and feelings in the manner of describing a 'lover's mind and heart'. Similar metaphors are used, similar conventional statements are repeated, 'Only he who is in love knows the rasa of love'. As he admires the splendour of Padmavati's quarters he thinks to himself, 'How splendidly beautiful the resident of this palace would be?'

He is apparently in the pain of 'love'. He is making efforts as well; after all, the truce offered to Ratansen is an 'effort' in itself. He is indeed suffering deeply due to his intense desire. But Jayasi has already ensured that his desire sounds hollow by placing the nature of Alauddin's 'desire' and 'efforts' in a wider perspective and in comparison with that of Ratansen.

Alauddin is feeling the 'pain of love' very deeply, but even at this moment, the idea of knowing Padmavati's own feelings does not cross his mind even for a moment. There is not a single word to indicate any anxiety in his mind, 'Does she desire, or even like me?' Her desire is absolutely of no consequence, as far as Alauddin is concerned. His 'love' is as hollow as is his offer of truce.

The feast is spread out. There is festive joviality all around. But Gora and Badal—the two great warriors of Chittor—are perturbed with the very idea of believing Alauddin's word. Having him in the inner chambers of the palace is ominous to them. They are apprehensive and caution the king to be careful of the Sultan. Ratansen is quite unhappy with them and preaches the virtue of having faith in 'nature's law' of good begetting good. He tells them not to think negatively of the Sultan, as negativity only breeds negativity. The warriors, irritated with this 'inane nobility', sullenly leave the feast and withdraw from the whole affair.

Dozens of beautiful maidens are serving the guests. Alauddin discretely asks Raghav Chetan to point out Padmini. He tells him, 'None of them even touches her shadow. They are just maids, beautiful of course, but their beauty fades in her presence like dimmed light of stars in the presence of a bright moon.'

With the meals, desserts and sherbets over, the Sultan doesn't seem to be in a hurry to leave. He proposes a game of chess, hoping for a glimpse of Padmavati.

A glimpse of Padmini

At this point, you may be wondering how the Sultan got a glimpse of Padmini and if the purported story of her image being shown in a mirror is 'true'.

Before answering this question, it is crucial to note that the answer from history is a 'no'. It just cannot be, as the whole affair of Padmini is simply *not* present in contemporary and later chronicles. For writing the narrative of history, sources such as inscriptions, chronicles, official documents and declarations are considered more trustworthy, as inspite of some exaggeration to glorify the concerned king, they are essentially 'factual'. For example, according to the court chronicles, the siege of Chittor lasted only for some months, as the Sultan was perturbed by reports of Mongol invasions and retreated to Delhi. Jayasi's poetic imagination stretches the siege to eight years and only hints at

some problem back home; just as it makes Alauddin's trusted warrior and emissary Sarja ride a lion and carry a serpent as a whip!

So the question, 'How did he get a glimpse of Padmini?' and others similar ones, can neither be asked nor answered from a 'historical' point of view.

These questions are to be placed and sensitively dealt with, in the twilight zone of legend, history and literary imagination. In other words, you can only compare Jayasi's account with those available in legends of Rajputana. And, the question then ought to be, 'How did *Jayasi's Alauddin* get a glimpse of Padmini?', 'In what way was it different from the manner in which the others have described it? Or, 'How and why *Jayasi's* Ratansen agreed?'

Well, Jayasi's Ratansen did not agree to any such thing. Jayasi does not even mention Ratansen and Alauddin discussing the idea of her glimpse or a reflection in a mirror.

As mentioned earlier, Jayasi got his story idea from the 'Padmini of Simhal' legends of Rajasthan. He developed both the Simhal and Chittor part of his story using his poetic imagination. He shifted the focus. He turned the *Gora Badal ri Chupai* or *Gora Badal ri Baat* of the warriors Gora and Badal into the epic of Padmavati. He gave unprecedented space to Nagmati's voice and crucially transformed Ratansen's character. From an ordinary king, Jayasi transformed him into the tragic hero of a poignant tale of love; a character in an epic which extends from the land of fables to the land of reality.

As we know, both the versions of the Padmini legend from Rajasthan were written down only after *Padmavat*; *Chupai* by Hemratan in 1588, and *Baat* by Jatmal in 1627. But from these texts, we certainly get an idea of the legends Jayasi might have heard. Both focus on the heroism of Gora and Badal; Ratansen and Padmini are there to put this heroism in bold relief. In Jatmal's *Baat*, Ratansen comes across as a particularly weak-kneed character.

It is in Jatmal's account that Ratansen gives in to Alauddin's demand of wanting a glimpse of Padmini. She is not comfortable with the idea and puts a maid in her place, beautiful enough to please the Sultan. But Raghav Chetan tells Alauddin that he has been taken for a ride. Alauddin 'complains' to Ratansen who then 'very angrily scolds Padmini for deceiving the Sultan' and orders her to show herself to Alauddin. Padmini shows her face from the oriel window, which has the expected effect on Alauddin, who now wants to go back to his camp. He praises 'brother' Ratansen for the nicety:

कोप कियो राजान कहइ पदमन प्रति अइसइ।
मुख दिखाउ अब वेग कपट मंड्उ तउ कइसइ॥
मुख काढ्यो पदमावती जाम बारी तइ बाहर।
निखि गिड्यउ सुलतान थांभ लीनउ त सुथाहर॥
खिण एक संभालइ आप कूँ साह कहइ देरइ चलउ।
क्या सिफत करूँ हूँ राय की रतनसेन भाई भलउ॥ —66
(see, *Rani Padmini* by Brajendra Kumar Singhal, Vani Prakashan: Delhi, 2017, p. 185).

Jatmal's Ratansen is a greedy man who receives baksheesh from the Sultan before being captured and tortured in captivity. From captivity, he sends a message to the fort asking Padmini to be sent to the Sultan so that his ordeal is over.

Hemratan's Ratansen fares better. In this account, he accedes to the Sultan's request of Padmini herself serving the meal in the truce feast. Padmini agrees to cook the food, but refuses to come before Alauddin to serve it.

Remember, Hemratan's Ratansen was provoked to get a 'padmini of Simhal' by the sarcasm of his first wife, Prabhavati, when he had one day complained about the quality of food cooked by her. So, Padmini, in this account is not only an enchanting beauty, but also a splendid cook. Jayasi, however, despite showing great interest in the art of cooking and cuisines does not attribute any great culinary skills to his Padmavati. She is more inclined towards scholarly pursuits.

According to Hemratan, during the feast, Alauddin is confused about the women serving the food. He wants to know which one is Padmini. Raghav tells him, 'It is not that easy to see her. The only way is to capture Ratansen and demand her as ransom.' In the meantime, Padmini, out of sheer curiosity, comes to the oriel window to take a look at the Sultan. (She does the same in Jayasi's account as well.) Raghav points her out to the Sultan who loses consciousness due to this brief glimpse. Ratansen is arrested when he comes out of the fort to see the Sultan off. Then the ransom demand is made, 'If you want Ratansen alive, send Padmini.' Veerbhan, Ratansen's son from his first wife, sees this as an opportunity to get rid of the woman who came as his mother's misfortune. Padmini, in order to avoid the calamity, seeks help from Gora and Badal (see *Padmavat* edited by Dr. Mata Prasad Gupta, Hindustani Academy: Allahabad, 1973, pp. 22–23).

Jayasi reworked the legends he had heard to suit his creative purpose. His Ratansen is not weak-kneed or greedy. He accepts Alauddin's truce offer, but *there is absolutely no question of a 'request' from Alauddin to get a glimpse of Padmavati as far as Jayasi's narration is concerned.* Going by Ratansen's character as created by Jayasi, it is understandable that any such 'request' would be rejected with contempt and the proposed truce would be put off. As a brave yet pragmatic king, Jayasi's Ratansen agrees to part with the 'invaluable five'; but does not accept even a reference to his wife. On the other hand, as an honourable man, he takes the Sultan's word on face value and scolds Gora and Badal for their 'negativity'. He is shown to suffer for his human qualities, not due to cowardice or greed. Even when in captivity, he suffers torture in dignified silence. In Chittor too, nobody even thinks of trading Padmini for Ratansen in Jayasi's *Padmavat.*

Jayasi, a devout Muslim, a revered Sufi and great poet of the 'pain of love', transformed a Hindu king into a memorable tragic hero of his epic; just like the Hindu poets of *Chhitai Charit*, half a century before Jayasi, gave Alauddin a humane touch and a fatherly persona with reference to Chhitai.

Both *Padmavat* and *Chhitai Charit* were composed not in order to celebrate the valour of any community or glorify any social identity, but to explore the aspects of human emotions of desire and love.

In Jayasi's narrative, Alauddin proposes a game of chess. It seems he has some intuition or hope that Padmavati will be interested to look at the emperor being hosted by her husband. When they sit down for chess, Alauddin discreetly arranges the nearby mirror in such a way that if and when Padmavati comes to the oriel window, her image will be in his view. Far from agreeing to facilitate Padmavati's glimpse, Jayasi's Ratansen is not even aware of Alauddin's manoeuvre.

At the same time, Padmavati's companions suggest that she should at least have a look at the emperor. These are young maidens, naturally excited to see such an important person around. They are glamour-stricken and describe his personality and power in superlatives. They prod the queen and tell her that never again will the emperor of Delhi visit Chittor: 'You also have a look, Padmavati, so that you don't regret the missed opportunity':

> (पातसाहि ढीली कर कत चितउर महँ आव।
> देखि लेहि पदुमावति हियँ न रहै पछिताव॥) —756

What a striking irony the poet creates by using the expression, 'regret' (पछिताव)!

She is encouraged to take a look at the emperor to avoid any future regret. Little does she know that she will end up regretting this one moment until the end of her life. And no Hiraman is around at this fraught turn of destiny to caution her. Padmavati, the epitome of unblemished beauty from the land of perfection, herself negotiates a momentous fallout in this land of perfidy, with success finally eluding her. The Simhal astrologers' forecast will come true. Padmavati will be 'taken by Yama in Jambudweep'.

This is the stuff tragedies are made of; one has to suffer without any fault on one's part.

Unaware of what fate has in store, the young queen comes giggling to the oriel window, and Alauddin finally catches a glimpse of her reflection in the mirror. Mesmerized, he not only loses the game of chess but also loses consciousness. Only Raghav Chetan, the perfidious pundit, and the mind behind the conspiracy, knows the real reason and he assures everyone, 'Nothing to worry, the emperor seems to have just chewed some bad betel.'

The emperor sleeps in the fort that night. In the morning, he recalls the wonder of the beauty which now seems like a dream to him. He cannot get over it and tells his confidant Raghav, 'I would prefer to be mauled by a tiger if I cannot get her.'

In yet another poetic master stroke, Jayasi without specifying who thought of the idea first, only informs us, 'It was decided (between the Sultan and Raghav Chetan) what is to be done next...'

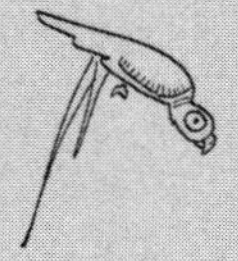

Chapter 5

'Ram and Sita Both Disappear'

Ratansen's ordeal and Devpal's depravity

Not much is known from the chronicles and other records about the fate of the ruler of Chittor, Rawal Ratansingh, who becomes Ratansen in *Padmavat.* We have already seen that in the *Chupai* and *Baat* tales of Gora and Badal, he is freed from captivity by these heroic warriors, and along with Padmavati, he blesses them. According to some sources, he meets his end in the battle, but some Jain sources also report him being arrested and taken away from Chittor by Alauddin. On all these matters, just as on the historicity of Padmini of Simhal, the jury is still out. But let us confine ourselves to Jayasi's narrative.

Jayasi tells us that Ratansen comes out of his fort, leaving his guards behind. The Sultan's hand is on his shoulder in the manner of an old friend, before he captures him. Jayasi puts Alauddin's cunning in a telling metaphor, 'He gave Ratansen poison in the garb of nectar.' Alauddin leaves for Delhi, taking Ratansen as a prisoner and sending shock waves throughout Chittor: 'Today, the sun has set in the daytime itself, darkness has overtaken Chittor' (आजु सूर दिन अंथवा, भा चितउर अँधियार।) —576.

A great poet need not announce the right and wrong of every situation in so many words; his challenge is to create situations and convey what he wants to. Jayasi meets this challenge of greatness brilliantly. Ratansen is brutally tortured and humiliated. Special torturers are assigned for him who torment him day and night, constantly reminding him of the great power of the Sultan. He is given a clear and cruel choice—hand over Padmavati or...

A defiant silence is the only response the tormentors get from their prisoner.

Jayasi demonstrates fascinating poetic ability in this episode. Each and every stanza describing the power and prestige of Alauddin resonates in the reader's mind as a testimony to the moral strength and valour of Ratansen. We are informed that along with people and kings in the vicinity of Chittor, places as far off as Khurasan (Iran) in the north and Bidar (Karnataka) in the south, are in awe of Sultan Alauddin. And why?

Because they can hardly believe that he has captured a king as brave and powerful as Ratansen of Chittor! By reporting it this way, Jayasi ensures the awe and prestige of the Sultan of Delhi is read as a tribute to the personality and character of Jayasi's hero.

Acharya Anandwardhana, the great Sanskrit theoretician of poetry, would call it a brilliant deployment of dhwani—the meaning which resonates beyond, sometimes even opposite, to the one visible. That is the exact case here.

Jatmal's Ratansen is tortured in prison and breaks down pitifully. He sends a message to Chittor asking for Padmini to be sent to the Sultan. To him, his Padmini is merely a queen (maybe one of many), even if she is the most beautiful. Jayasi's Ratansen, however, is a resplendent study in contrast—a portrait of courage, patience and integrity. He suffers all the humiliation and indignities in a dignified silence. To him, his Padmavati is not one of many queens, but his true love. She is more than his life—just like for the reader, she is more than real.

While in Simhal, Jayasi's Ratansen had laughingly remarked, 'Like Mansur' (the great Sufi martyr), when he was being taken for execution. Here, he suffers in silence with the equanimity of a yogi. Life has taught him the hard way: 'Grief burns you, it roasts you; it is deadlier than the vajra (the ultimate weapon of Indra, the king of devas). It takes away your sense of shame (i.e. honour). Only he who has suffered, knows what grief can do' :

(दुख जारै, दुख भुँजै, दुख खोवै सब लाज।
गाजहि चाहि गरुब दुख दुखी जान जेहि बाज॥) —581

But Ratansen has not lost his sense of honour at all. He has not even been defeated honourably on the battlefield. He has been taken prisoner by betrayal and deceit. Alauddin, by using dishonourable cunning to overpower him, has conceded defeat in the contest of love and honour.

You can hear Mansur's defiant laughter in the background of the equanimous silence of Ratansen—the love-yogi.

Back home in Chittor, 'overtaken by darkness'; there is natural lamentation all around. Both Padmavati and Nagmati are deeply grieved; and Jayasi makes Padmavati put a philosophical gloss on her and Nagmati's loss: 'Where do I find you, my dear? How can I find you anywhere outside, when you reside in my heart?':

(कवन खंड हौ हेरौं कहाँ मिलहु हो नाहँ।
हेरें कतहुँ न पावौं बसहु तौ हिरदैं माहँ॥) —583

It is a great statement of self-realization, echoing Kabir and others. In the present context, however, this 'realization' of your loved one (human or God) residing in your heart only adds to the melancholy of the situation in an ironical way.

Jayasi is now coming closer to the finale of his story. Ratansen dies, but Jayasi will not let him die at the hands of Alauddin. It would take away from his superior status, a prospect Jayasi is not ready to allow. He introduces Devpal of Kumbhalner (an imaginary character) to avoid this prospect.

Devpal has had designs on Padmavati for long. Now, he takes Ratansen's calamity as an opportunity. He sends a dooti to seduce Padmavati.

The word 'dooti' is the feminine form of doot—an emissary or a messenger—as in the famed *Meghdoot* by Kalidasa, wherein a yaksha exiled from his country requests the megh (cloud) to act as a messenger and take his message to his beloved.

But unlike doot, the term dooti carries a negative connotation in Indian literature and folklore. She is not exactly a procuress. She is not formally in the 'profession'. She is like the woman-next-door, leading a regular social life. But known only to a select few is her other side. She seduces women for the powerful and is rewarded handsomely for her 'services'. She, perforce, has to have the capacity of winning over the unsuspecting maidens by tricks of confidence. Expertise in spells and charms are a dooti's additional qualifications.

The dooti deputed by Devpal is an old Brahmin woman named Kumudini, an expert in all the 'arts' of a dooti, and very confident too. She prepares to leave for Chittor with her experience and knowledge: 'The body ages, not the mind; desire continues to haunt even a frail body.' Summing up her reflections, Jayasi himself adds, 'What is an old person walking with a bent body, with his/her gaze caste down, looking for? Obviously the jewel of youth s/he has lost':

> (मुहमद बिरिंध जो नै चलै काह चलै भुइँ टोइ।
> जोबन रतन हेरान है मकु धरती महँ होइ ॥) —586

She reaches Chittor and introduces herself as the daughter of Gandharvsen's (Padmavati's father) priest, who had 'fed Padmavati in her lap'.

Here, paradoxically, we see both the strength and weakness of the poet. First his strength. In literature and folklore a married Indian woman nurtures a soft corner for her parental home (maika) all her life. This soft corner continues even when she has become a matriarch herself. In moments of happiness and distress, she expects the presence of her parental home in some way or another. We have recalled the tragic death of Sati (Shiva's consort) who could not resist the temptation to attend a ceremony at her father's place, even uninvited. This dooti knows that in this situation of distress, Padmavati will easily open up to someone from home. And, somebody from the maika never comes empty-handed; so our senior citizen 'from Simhal' also brings a number of delicious dishes along.

True to his tremendous knowledge of cultural practices, the

delicacies Jayasi mentions in this context (maath, pheni, laddus) are exactly those which are still sent by parents in Rajasthan and northern India to their married daughters.

But here emerges the weakness of a 'poet in a hurry', which Jayasi has certainly become by now. Padmavati not only opens up to the woman, but does so without any inhibition as a woman of the royal household. She cries bitterly, falling into the old woman's lap. She complains, 'Why did my parents give me life, if I were to suffer all this? Why did God not end my life in childhood itself?' She curses herself: 'How shameless of me, my husband rots in prison and I am living in this palace.'

But not even once does it strike the poet to have Padmavati complain about the absolute absence of any help from her parental side during her husband's confrontation with the Sultan of Delhi and its calamitous aftermath.

The poetic structure demanded that the poet maintained the consistency of total absence of Simhal in the narrative after Padmavati's marriage, and should have made Kumudini claim some other place as her native one. Otherwise, Simhal should have been present in the narrative throughout.

Jayasi could not miss the emotive potential of 'someone from the parental home in a moment of distress'; but did not have the either the time or the inclination to take care of the resultant Simhal-related inconsistency in the post-wedding narrative structure.

Kumudini, the dooti, proceeds in her task very carefully. She first reminds the young maiden of the transience of youth and the need to enjoy the erotic pleasures, as, 'youth is quite ruthless too, once gone, it is never back again.' Once it passes, 'your body, as taut as an arrow today, will be left bent like a bow' (छरिक जाइहि बान लै धनुक छाँड़ि तोहि हाथ)—593. 'Why waste youth? Why ignore erotic desire? Why not enjoy it, as long as you are young?'—This is the message of the dooti.

Padmavati is clever enough to get to the bottom of the dooti's 'philosophizing', and responds furiously, 'Enjoy, yes, but only with my own man'. Kumudini, the dooti, is undeterred, and unhesitatingly suggests 'a change of taste': 'You are a lotus,' she says, 'why limit the flavour of your fragrance to only one? Why not try other bumblebees as well?' Padmavati gets more disgusted and furious, and now Kumudini compares the calamity of Ratansen with the 'riches and pomp of Devpal', whose Kumbhalner makes one forget even Chittor.

Padmavati has had enough by now, 'How dare you compare that lowly person with my beloved?' She also recalls Raghav Chetan: 'You are as villainous as him!' She orders a good thrashing of Kumudini, the dooti!

After a short while, she has to suffer another dooti—this time from Alauddin himself. The dooti from Devpal had posed as a Brahmin woman; but this one has come in the garb of a jogin (a female yogi). The reason is simple—Brahmins and yogis were respected and had easy access to common households as well as royal palaces.

This dooti from Delhi has a devious brief. She has been instructed to 'convert' Padmavati into a jogin and bring her to Delhi. She describes the plight of Ratansen in the Sultan's custody and implicitly asks Padmavati to join her as a jogin. Padmavati is almost taken in by her sweet talk, but is cautioned by her companions who advise her to approach Gora and Badal for consolation and genuine help.

The dooti from Delhi fails to take Padmavati along, but she leaves behind a nugget of wisdom, which was true then and is true now. Delhi, the capital, the centre of political power, was called Dheeli those days, and this word literally means—loose. The jogin dooti tells Padmavati, 'Dheeli is Dheeli (loose) only in name, in practice; it never loosens its grip!' (ढीली नाउँ न जानहिं ढीली। सुठि बँदि गाढ़ न निकसै कीली ॥) —604.

Is it not true of political power always and everywhere?

The dooti episode takes the story ahead, but its real import lies in reinforcing Jayasi's healthy world view.

Jayasi celebrates youth. We will soon see that he hates the idea of himself living the life of a frail old man. He composed his magnum opus to celebrate love and desire; he is in love with good food; but he is not given to crass and gross pleasure-seeking. He is not a hedonist.

His *Padmavat* is certainly not a Sufi allegory, and it is also not an advocacy for hedonism. His Padmavati has a healthy approach to erotic pleasure. Completely free of any prudishness of approach to love, desire and sex, she is equally hateful of manipulation in these matters. Her view can be summed up thus:

'Erotic pleasure is not a sin at all, the body is not something to be ashamed of; it ought to be nurtured and celebrated. But this cannot be done with base motives like extracting money out of a king or any powerful man. I will indulge my desires of erotic and other enjoyments only with the man I really admire and love. I will share his sufferings as well. I am not one of those women who seduce or get seduced by men with power and discard them as soon as they are out of power.'

The heroism of Gora and Badal

Advised by her friends, Padmavati approaches the sullen warriors Gora and Badal. We do not get any hint of any other person or any war-council in Chittor thinking of ways to free the captured king. In bardic accounts, Padmavati approaches Gora and Badal when Ratansen himself breaks down (Jatmal), or when Veerbhan is planning to get rid of her (Hemratan).

Jayasi is not interested in these details. *His* Ratansen in any case does not act in this cowardly fashion. Following the dictates of his poetic logic of maintaining the consistency of characters crafted by him, Jayasi skips these details of the legend completely.

The warriors Gora and Badal were indeed honourable men. Finding the crying queen at their doorstep, they tremble as 'never before'. They recall their suspicion of the Sultan's motives and Ratansen chiding them for the same. But, now, Padmavati—the queen—herself has come to them. They 'wipe dust from her feet with their hair' and ask her to order them.

Jayasi's Padmavati is not merely a 'desirable' woman, or a passive nayika (heroine) of romance. She is a woman of substance. While in Simhal, she had challenged her suitor Ratansen to prove himself worthy of her. Now, she is here, but not to request the warriors to do something; she already has a plan.

She is clever enough not to think of a frontal confrontation with the mighty Sultan, but what she has in mind is not very feasible: 'I will go myself as a jogin and free my beloved, even if I am taken prisoner myself' (पिय जहँ बंदि जोगिन होइ धावौं। हौं होइ बंदि पियहि मोकरावौं)—609.

Alauddin could not have wished for more. But maybe she is confident that once freed, her beloved will be too much for the

Sultan. Gora and Badal, the seasoned warriors and the loyal 'servants' cannot even think of letting her do such a thing. The point, however, is her resolve.

Now, the warriors are shedding 'tears of blood'. 'The king did not listen to us,' they recall, 'that is why, we were angry and withdrawn. The "turk" should have been arrested in the palace itself. But that is in the past now. How can we let you go as a jogin? Just wait for the rainy season to end, your grief will also be over. We will free the sun from his eclipse and bring him to the moon.'

Padmavati, in her grateful praise of the two warriors, places them in the company of many mythological and legendary heroes. Of particular interest here is the allusion to Hanuman's act of freeing Ram and Laksman from from the clutches of Mahiravan: (जस हनिवँत राघौ बँदि छोरी। तस तुम्ह छोरि मिलावहु जोरी॥) —611.

This story is found in the Bengali Ramayan by Krittiwas, and also in the *Anand Ramayan*, a post-Tulsidas text of undetermined authorship. In this story, Ravan, after losing his son Meghnad in battle, is very depressed and seeks help from his brother Mahiravan, who succeeds in abducting Ram and Laksman from their camp. He intends to sacrifice them to the goddess. Only Hanuman can help save the situation; he goes to Mahiravan's land; Ram and Laksman are freed and Mahiravan himself is sacrificed to the goddess.

Though not found in *Ramcharitmanas*, this story is still enacted in the Ramlilas across northern India.

Gora and Badal assure Padmavati and wish her and her husband eternal bliss. Hearing these words and Ratansen's name being mentioned with reassuring confidence, 'Padmavati feels like a lotus looking at the sun. These words of saffron hue reached her heart' (सुनि सूरज कवँलहि जिय जागा। केसरि बरन बोल हियँ लागा॥) —612.

Gora and Badal's good wish is simply ironical and tragic. The colour saffron signifies pleasure and romance as well as sacrifice. Her pleasure on hearing these words is a portent of the impending sacrifice of Gora, and later on, of her own disappearance along with Ratansen and Nagmati.

Gora and Badal are always mentioned in the legend as a duo, implying a deep bond of friendship and togetherness. They were indeed great friends, but, while Gora was a middle-aged man, Badal was his nephew—a recently wed young lad. In fact, it was the time of his gauna, when the marriage is actually consummated. His decision to join his uncle shocks and saddens his family. His mother Yashodevi is devastated and so is his wife, who has just arrived from her parental home. His mother tells him about the frightening power of the mighty Sultan of Delhi and reminds him

of his wife and the long life that awaits the young couple. His wife hopes to impress him with her charms and invites him to join the 'battle of lovemaking' instead of the one with deadly arms.

Badal, the young warrior and a man of honour, is unimpressed. Underlining the similarity of her name to that of Lord Krishna's mother, he says: 'Don't think too much of the Sultan's might. You are Yashoda and I, your son, am capable of taking on any enemy, going anywhere to achieve my goal.' To the expectant young bride, the warrior's message is, 'This is no time for shringara; this is a moment of vira.'

Indian poetics presume nine aesthetic emotions (rasas). *Shringara* stands for the erotic and *vira* for the heroic. With his word of honour given to his queen involved, the pleas of the young warrior's newly-wed are not going to work.

The warriors plan their strategy. Padmavati's plan of going to Delhi is mentioned as another proof of inferior intelligence of women in their discussion, and yet, it is this plan that actually gives an idea to superiorly intelligent men!

Gora and Badal are great warriors, but also clever enough to know the difference between boastful hyperboles and harsh realities. They are willing to bravely lay down their lives for a worthy purpose, but are not moronic to commit suicide in the name of honour and tradition or some other empty slogan. In the given situation, they realize that, 'Man has to use deceit in order to make up for lack of force; depending on the situation one has to sometimes act as a flower, and sometime as a thorn':

(पुरुख तहाँ करै छर जहँ बर कीन्हें न आँट।
जहाँ फूल तहाँ फूल होई, जहां काँट तहाँ काँट ॥) —621

The plan is executed in utmost secrecy. Sixteen hundred palanquins carrying armed warriors are organized. In one of these, an ironsmith is seated (to break Ratansen's prison irons) so secretively that even the 'sun is not aware'. The word is spread that Padmavati has ultimately decided to submit to the Sultan's command and is leaving for Delhi along with her servants and companions. Some ceremonial guards led by Gora and Badal are accompanying this procession of 'royal ladies'.

Shortly before the procession reaches Delhi, Gora has already bribed the incharge of the prison where Ratansen is being held. This man has agreed to request the Sultan to allow Padmavati's brief meeting with her captive husband so that she can hand over the key to Chittor Fort to him. Having done this, she will immediately reach the Sultan's place as desired. The Sultan agrees to this request.

Something quite interesting is emerging here. Apparently, Alauddin is not bent upon taking Chittor under his direct charge. He expects Padmavati to come to his harem, and Ratansen, pocketing the humiliation and the key to his fort, to go back to Chittor as Alauddin's vassal.

Bribed handsomely, the prison guards don't even bother to check the palanquins carrying the 'royal ladies' and let them pass through to the prison campus; giving Jayasi an opportunity here to comment on greed, bribe and corruption, 'Bribe is the river of greed and sin, anybody dipping hands in it loses the essence. The servants seeking and getting bribes start "ruling" themselves and harm their master':

(लोभ पाप कै नदी अँकोरा। सतु न रहै हाथ जस बोरा॥
जहँ अँकोर तहँ नेगिन्ह राजू। ठाकुर केर बिनासहिं काजू॥) —624

The ironsmith releases the king, who gets battle-ready in no time and joins the 'warriors in the palanquins'. Badal asks Gora to proceed towards Chittor taking Ratansen along, and proposes to hold back the Sultan's army. Gora returns the offer, pointing out, 'I have lived my life and you have just started yours.' He stays back to hold the Sultan's army, after sending Badal along with Ratansen.

Gora fights valiantly, in fact, ferociously; in the end, only Sarja—Alauddin's incomparable warrior riding a lion and carrying a serpent as a whip—is able to take him on. Gora has to die, but he has achieved his goal. His king is safely on his way back to Chittor. His face was 'blackened' when his lord was taken in custody by deceit. Now, having released him, he has washed his face with blood and brought back its hue and shine:

> (रतनसेनि तुम्ह बाँधा मसि गोरा के गात।
> जब लग रुधिर न धौवों तब लगि होउँ न रात॥) —634

In the versions of the story by Hemratan and Jatmal, Gora and Badal occupy the centre stage. Gora's wife commits sati with his headgear in her lap. He along with his surviving nephew receive the blessings of the grateful royal couple. Jayasi's Padmavati also expresses her gratitude to Badal when he reaches Chittor along with Ratansen. Having received her husband and touched his feet, she performs aarti on Badal. 'You have saved the honour of my vermilion,' she tells Badal and worships his horse in the customary way. The elephants and horses of the household are worshipped on Dussera. This is the Dussera day for Padmavati and all of Chittor.

Jayasi has put Padmavati in the centre of his version, but has not forgotten to pay Gora and Badal their due. His Gora dies in the battlefield sending his head 'as an example of bravery to the Sultan; Badal accompanies Ratansen back to Chittor':

(गोरा परा खेत महँ सिर पहुँचावा बान।
बादिल लै गा राजहिं लै चितउर नियरान ॥) —637

...And all this comes to an end

Having participated in the welcoming celebration for Ratansen, the lovers are finally with each other. Sadly, Nagmati is completely missing from the account beginning with the attempts to free Ratansen until this point. She only reappears in the wake of Ratansen's demise.

The couple exchange memories of their sufferings and torments. Giving chilling details of what he had to suffer, Ratansen tells Padmavati, 'Only the faint, yet insistent hope of seeing you again kept me alive, otherwise it was impossible to survive the torture, solitude and humiliation.'

Padmavati also cannot hold back her experience of Devpal's advances through the dooti. She recalls telling this dooti, 'Just as fire is implicitly present in wood, so is my husband within me.' Ratansen instantly leaves to teach Devpal a lesson, telling himself, 'I will be worthy of being known as Ratansen, only if I get hold of him before the Turks reach Chittor' (जब लग आइ तुरुक गढ़ बाजा। तब लगि धरि आनौं तौ राजा ॥)—645.

This is an attempt on the poet's part to save his hero from being defeated by Alauddin. His Padmavati does not wait even for a day to let Ratansen know about Devpal. Whatever may be the historical fact, in Jayasi's narrative, Alauddin is bound to follow Ratansen to Chittor and the outcome of the ensuing conflict can very well be imagined. In a poignant poetic move, he makes Padmavati an instrument to facilitate Ratansen's honourable demise.

The next morning itself, Kumbhalner is surrounded by Ratansen's forces. Devpal responds by challenging Ratansen to a duel instead of engaging their respective armies (perhaps yet another device to bring the narrative to end as soon as possible). Devpal attacks Ratansen and fatally wounds him. Ratansen's counter-attack cuts Devpal, but he is not going to survive for long himself.

Padmavati's warrior is brought home half-dead.

Ratansen hands over Chittor to Badal and the gods leave his body.

Now in the next three stanzas, Jayasi describes Padmavati and Nagmati's resolve and preparations for sati on their husband's pyre, and he undoubtedly does so with admiration for their love and commitment to their man, noting, 'the wives who have been competing and quarrelling for the husband's favours are sitting side by side and will leave the world together as satis.'

But, as mentioned earlier, he gives exactly three words to report jauhar, (*jauhar bhain istiry...*)—absolutely no admiration here.

The pyre is lit, and...

'As they were committing sati, the Shah's forces surrounded the fort. But it was too late for them. Ram and Sita had disappeared.

The Shah came and heard all the details with regret, "I wanted to avoid all this, but could not." He picked a handful of ashes from the pyre (and continued):

The desire remains insatiable and permanent
But this world is just illusionary and transient
Insatiable desire man continues to have
Till life is over and he reaches his grave.

The battle continues. Badal also perishes. Women commit jauhar, men die in the battle. The Sultan destroys the fort, Chittor is overtaken by Islam.'

(ओइ सह गवन भईं जब ताईं। पातसाहि गढ़ छेंका आई॥
तब लगि सो औंसर होइ बीता। भए अलोप राम औ सीता॥
आइ साहि सब सुना अखारा। होइ गा राति देवस जो बारा॥
छार उठाइ लीन्हि एक मूँठी। दीन्हि उड़ाइ पिरथिमी झूठी॥
जो लगि ऊपर छार न परई। तब लगि नाहिं जो तिस्ना मरई॥
सगरै कटक उठाई माँटी। पुल बाँधा जहँ जहँ गढ़ घाटी॥
भा ढोवा भा जूझि असूझा। बादिल आइ पँवरि होइ जूझा॥
जौहर भईं इस्तिरी पुरुख भए संग्राम।
पातसाहि गढ़ चूरा चितउर भा इसलाम॥) —651

In the descriptions of the court chronicles, this is naturally a moment of celebration, but the poet turns this victory into a pyrrhic one. Jayasi's Alauddin feels weighed down (if only momentarily) with the moral guilt of having caused such a devastation only because of his infatuation. In fact, *this realization belongs to the poet only*, who is however realistic enough to immediately describe the continuation of war and the final capture of Chittor.

But, by making Alauddin the victor and the medium of his

rather depressing reflections, Jayasi makes it absolutely impossible for anyone to celebrate his victory over Chittor.

The finale of his great epic resonates not with the celebration of victory, but with a sad report: 'Ram and Sita have disappeared.'

The end of this tale, exploring desire in its many aspects, also resonates with the memory of something that Bhartrihari had said some centuries before. He is also mentioned in *Padmavat* as a great yogi; he was a great poet and a great theoretician of language as well. He reminds us the inevitable truth, 'The time does not pass, only we pass away/ the desire never withers, only we wither away' (कालो न यातो वयमेव याता/ तृष्णा न जीर्णा वयमेव जीर्णा:).

Jayasi's epilogue

All great poets, perforce, deal with, in fact, are obsessed with two primary facts of life—love and death. Jayasi is no exception, as we have seen. He has put love and life in an ultimate existential perspective of transience in the context of death. Jayasi's moving description of the final moment of this story of erotic desire, endeavour, fulfilment, destruction and death is a stroke of poetic genius. What we hear at the end of his narration may or may not be true historically; but that is the truth of poetry—which the poet wants to share with you, and does it so poignantly that it moves a sensitive reader to tears.

The story over, Jayasi has something to say about his motive behind writing it. Also, rather unexpectedly, something about old age. These two stanzas are the last in the text. A third, supposedly providing a key to the 'Sufi allegory', has been dismissed by consensus amongst scholars as a much later extrapolation into *Padmavat.*

Jayasi puts his motive quite frankly and simply in the following moving words, remembering Hiraman also after such a long gap:

'Muhammad has composed this poem in blood and tears. One who listens to it will himself/herself be able to sing the torments of love; I created glue of my blood, and soaked it into my tears. I created this poem, thinking of leaving some sign behind. Where is now the king like Ratansen, where is Hiraman the parrot, who generated intelligence, where is Sultan Alauddin, and where is Raghav Chetan who described Padmavati to Alauddin, and where is the beautiful Queen Padmavati herself? Nothing but the story survives in the world. Blessed are those who earn renown, as the fragrance persists even after the flower has perished.

'Who in this world does not long for abiding fame?
I hope, the readers of this story will also remember my name.'

(मुहम्मद यहि कवि जोर सुनावा। सुना जो पेम पीर गा पावा॥
जोरी लाइ रकत कै लेई। गाढ़ी प्रीति नैन जल सोई॥
औ मन जानि कवित अस कीन्हा। मकु यह रहै जगत महँ चीन्हा॥
कहाँ सो रतनसेनि अस राजा। कहाँ सुवा असि बुधि उपराजा॥
कहाँ अलाउदीन सुलतानू। कहँ राघौ जेइँ कीन्ह बखानू॥
कहँ सुरुप पदुमावति रानी। कोइ न रहा जग रही कहानी॥
धनि सो पुरुख जस कीरति जासू। फूल मरै पै मरै न बासू॥
केइँ न जगत जस बेंचा केइँ न लीन्ह जस मोल।
जो यह पढ़ै कहानी हम सँवरै दुइ बोल॥) —652

Is there even a trace here of hope to convert you to Sufism or any 'ism' for that matter? The poet does not even want himself to be remembered as a great Sufi. No hint of any ambition in the area of miracles either. He is unpretentious about his 'desire'—which in any case is a universal one. Everyone wants to live on in memories, so does the poet of *Padmavat*.

The last stanza of *Padmavat* is not about the key to Sufi allegory, but about the horrors of old age. One is not sure, if the poet composed it when he had really grown old, or he had just imagined old age and had come up with this distressing message:

'(Muhammad says), it is now old age, youth is left behind. Strength has left the body, vision has given way to mistiness in the eyes, face has shrunk, teeth are gone. The voice has turned hoarse. Clear thinking has given way to imbecility, the pride which held the head high has gone and head is bowed, the ears have lost hearing, hair has gone completely grey. The body is living, but as if dead, as youth has left it. Youth is life, if it is gone, you depend on others and dependence is as good as death.

'An old man shaking head is actually recalling and cursing those who blessed and wished him a very long life.'

(मुहमद बिरिध बएस अब भई। जोबन हुत सो अवस्था गई॥
बल जो गएउ कै खीन सरीरू। दिस्टि गई नैनन्ह दै नीरू॥
दसन गए कै तुचा कपोला। बैन गए दै अनरुचि बोला॥
बुद्धि गई हिरदै बौराई। गरब गएउ तरहुँड़ सिर नाई॥
सरवन गए ऊँच दै सुना। गारौ गएउ सीस भा धुना॥
भँवर गएउ केसन्ह दै भुवा। जोबन गएउ जियत जनु मुवा॥
तब लगि जीवन जोबन साथाँ। पुनि सो मींचु पराए हाथाँ॥
बिरिध जो सीस डोलावै सीस धुनै तेहि रीस।
बूढ़े आढ़े होहु तुम्ह केइँ यह दीन्ह असीस॥) —653

Malik Muhammad Jayasi, frail, 'ugly' man, scholar, revered Sufi, was a poet of youth. He sang of love and its adventures. He sang of youthful enthusiasm and courage. He sang of the capacity to take challenges, even face death for something worthy. He also sang of friendship and loyalty.

He wanted not to live a long but decimated life physically. He desired an immortal life, and he ensured it through his creation—*Padmavat*.

Conclusion: An Antidote to Deformities

So nobody and nothing, except the story is left behind. This is as true of the characters as of the creator of *Padmavat.* And, of course of us, its readers as well. But, as we know, 'fragrance persists even after the flower has perished...'

Maybe, it would be a good idea to ask ourselves—what kind of fragrance are we left with, having gone through this reading of *Padmavat?*

As far as Jayasi is concerned, he composed *Padmavat* to celebrate human love—मानुष प्रेम—and to explore the ethics of desire. Both Ratansen and Alauddin desire the same woman, and probably with the same intensity. The difference lies in their approach.

Ratansen cannot even imagine the use of force to 'have' the desired woman. He first has to determine her own consent and willingness and then strive hard—not as an aggressor but as a yogi—a love-yogi. Alauddin, on the other hand cannot imagine any method other than force and aggression to fulfil his desire.

The point Jayasi's Padmavat *makes very forcefully is this—the consent and willingness of a woman is fundamentally important. It cannot be taken for granted. In a relationship of mutual desire and respect, all erotic acts and expressions are just natural, morally valid and aesthetically pleasant. In the absence of consent and willingness even the word 'love' sounds intrusive and uncalled for. Any man claiming to love a woman without bothering about her own desire, and trying to impose himself in an intrusive manner is giving way to the same indifference and arrogance which made Alauddin's attempts unacceptable ethically and aesthetically.*

It is important to constantly remember that Jayasi's Khalji is not a monster. His obsession with Padmavati coupled with his intoxication of power leads him to act in an immoral way in this particular context. However at the same time, Jayasi's Alauddin is not only a competent ruler but also a king who gives alms to the needy without bothering about their religious identity. He respects the Chittor sentiment of his Rajput vassals. His inner reflections on the vagaries of political power are coloured with the idiom and memories of Ram Katha.

Historically, Alauddin is credited with repulsing the Mongol invasions of India. Jayasi also indirectly hints at this fact. His Khalji, like any other character in the epic, is a product of his times. He is destined to play a negative role in this particular saga, but Jayasi is careful not to allow this negativity overshadow Alauddin's overall personality. He has not made him into a monster or an alien.

Jayasi clearly sides with his hero, Ratansen the love-yogi, not because of his social identity, but because of his individual sadhana. He is also a product of his times. The point, however, is that the poet makes him transcend the limit set by his times. He is a king, but is in a serious relationship with only two women. In Simhal, he is assured of all divine help if he decides to use force against Gandharvsen, but no, he insists, in matters of the heart, the force of arms has no place. Not only the love of his beloved, even the consent of her parents is to be obtained only and only by persuasion and perseverance.

Jayasi's Ratansen is a yogi not only in appearance, but in the process of love, he becomes a yogi in essence. He is committed to his own self, his love, his duties as husband, householder and of course, his responsibilities as a king.

Padmavati is 'divine' since her birth. As we saw, the poet goes into ecstasy even while describing her arrival. Ratansen, on the other hand, is a normal human being, who acquires great qualities of human character by his sadhana. He performs such great yoga that the greatest of the yogis, Mahadeva, himself helps him and gives him siddhi-gutika i.e. key to mysteries.

Ratansen's love-yoga is a great takeaway for male readers of Jayasi's *Padmavat*.

In Indian tradition, one world view upholds the life of the householder. It believes in the four-fold ideal of life—Dharma, Artha, Kama and Moksha. This implies earning your livelihood by righteous means and enjoying life's pleasure and then finally striving for liberation. On the other hand, there is a world view which seeks to exclusively focus on moksha or nirvana and holds those leading an ordinary life almost in contempt.

Jayasi's *Padmavat* makes a very powerful and creative intervention in this ongoing debate. His Ratansen performs yoga-sadhana in order to make himself worthy of the love of the woman who is at the centre of his desire. His yoga works for healthy and moral erotic desire, not against it. His yoga starts with the question—'What is the meaning of life, if you do not traverse the path of love, and do not take its challenges?' And his sadhana is rewarded with the realization that in fact, it is human love that transforms a man or a woman into something divine.

Having achieved the result of his sadhana, the love-yogi comes back to real life better prepared ethically and pragmatically to face it.

The question faced by Ratansen and the answer earned by him alludes to Jayasi's own experience. The poet had the 'first darshan' of love in Jayas, a little town which then became Jayasi's 'first garden'—the garden of paradise. He composed *Padmavat* to deeply and creatively reflect on the memories of his life and love. Being a poetic genius, he transformed his memories and reflections into an epic which went beyond his own life experience as well as his own lifetime. He composed it so that its reader or listener herself will also sing the 'pain of love'; and in the process, will probably remember the poet also a bit!

Jayasi took his theme from the legends and oral traditions, and developed it to suit his purpose. One 'innovation' he made in the legend is extremely important to understand his 'love statement' completely. Jayasi imagines Devpal and his attempts to seduce Padmavati by sending a dooti. Padmavati's disgusted and contemptuous rejection of the same is brought in to emphasize the integrity of love sentiment from Padmavati's point of view. Lovers cannot be fair-weather friends. Yes, body is great, its pleasures are not embarrassing but enjoyable, *but* not at the cost of human integrity and commitment.

This book has tried to take you on a conducted tour of Jayasi's masterpiece which in itself is a veritable garden of pleasures, as well as a terrain of poetic challenges. And, let me assure you, at no point in this tour, I have forgotten the time-distance between him and us. Nowhere have I tried to make Jayasi 'politically correct'. After all, like any human being he was a product of his times and it is absolutely pointless to expect that a poet of the sixteenth century would be exactly on the same page with us in the twenty-first century on matters like love, gender and social hierarchy.

The point is, Jayasi, the poet, transcends the limits of his historical times. All great poets, philosophers and thinkers do. That is why they are considered great.

And, it gives us an opportunity to reflect on something interesting, or shall we say, actually depressing. As you know by now, Jayasi, who is given to describing everything (from the kind of foods to the kind of horses and weapons) in such great detail, gives *exactly three words* to describe the custom of mass self-immolation by women.

And what do we see around us today? Supposedly educated, cultured people justifying, even glorifying 'jauhar' in the name of 'tradition'. Sadly, in our society these days, not just Jayasi's *Padmavat*, but also on other matters related to history, anachronism seems to be assuming epidemic proportions. *Anachronism works in two apparently conflicting, but actually complimenting ways, both equally harmful. You read jauhar and sati as if it is being recommended for today, and feel angry. Conversely, you read it, as it should prevail today and feel angry that it does not.*

Let Jayasi not be made co-culprit, if some 'artist' decides today to focus on and celebrate jauhar and its details using a lot of verbal or visual footage. One can only wish some aesthetic sense and moral responsibility to such an 'artist' and his/her fan club.

In any case, it would be stupid on Jayasi's part not to describe a custom (good or bad) at the appropriate moment; it is infinitely more stupid on our part to go back to the mindset of Jayasi's time and glorify jauhar and sati in our times. The sense of history implies recognizing the pastness of the past, and draw lessons from it for the future. In the absence of this sense of future, and a proper ethical perspective, sense of history does not take long in turning into nonsense of history!

Similarly, the debate about the historicity of *Padmavat* seems to be motivated not by a sense of history, but by a terror of it. What needs to be appreciated, in fact admired, about Jayasi's *Padmavat* is that it turned legend into something more important than history. It needs to be constantly borne in mind that contrary to what some people think, to Jayasi, the 'imaginary' is infinitely more important than 'historical'. More than two-thirds of his epic is devoted to happenings in the spheres of legendary and imaginary. The 'Sultan of Delhi' is referred to quite late in the narrative. Simhal is more important to Jayasi than Chittor and Delhi—which are just harsh foils to the tender and fabulous Simhal.

Most of the 'debate' around *Padmavat* seems unable to appreciate this basic point. It also seems unable to understand that history is about real people and events; but in the life of a community as well as that of an individual, there are some things, events and people which/who are more than real, and are crucially important precisely because of this. Maybe Padmavati was indeed a historical figure, maybe she was not; the jury of serious researchers is still out; but in Jayasi's epic, she is *much more than real.* She is not only a perfect beauty, but also an almost perfect human being. One can understand (with disagreement of course) those who in their reading of *Padmavat*, understand her as symbolizing God or Brahman—the Ultimate Reality.

Jayasi's *Padmavat* is an epic of conventional love, normal erotic desire, metamorphosing into something unique, something divine. His message if any, is that not of Sufism or of Rajput or Hindu honour but of erotic desire and love transforming human beings into the divine. If at all *Padmavat* has any spiritual content, it is that spirituality ought to be celebrated beyond religious denominations. It is about Kama—erotic desire—which takes you to Ram. It is also about celebrating the pleasures of life (including food!), but not being given to them at the cost of essential humanity and ethical obligations.

Jayasi's knowledge is vast, but unlike Tulsidas, he is rather narrowly focused on exploring aspects of love and desire.

He has a liberal temperament and implicitly conveys the need of transcending narrow social boundaries, insisting on the transformative power of love; but unlike Kabir, nowhere does he interrogate or problematize these boundaries as such.

Jayasi's epic is not about monsters on one side and deities on the other. Devpal, the depraved king who seeks to seduce Padmavati, is not a Turk and does not belong to any alien location. As a matter of fact, not even Padmavati—the perfect human being and beauty— is without some faults. The only *bad* one is Raghav Chetan and the only one without fault is Hiraman, who is not a human being—if human, you are a mixed package.

You have to earn guna (positive qualities and attitude) and work hard to sustain it.

Let us read *Padmavat* with sensitivity to the poet's own concerns, instead of reducing it to an artefact of our designs. Let us read it as a celebration of and a reflection on love, and refrain from making it a tool of rationalizing *our* misogynist fantasies of total control of a woman's mind and body.

Read as a creative foray into the themes of love and desire; transience and death; maybe *Padmavat* will act upon us also and make us realize the divine—Baikunthi—potential of human love.

Jayasi the poet was conscious of his bodily deformities and used poetry as an antidote. Are we willing to face the increasing deformities of our souls and minds? Are we blessed with any moral and aesthetic antidote, or just condemned to rush towards a fractured social psyche, an imbecile intellect and a violent society?